Self-Knowledge

Shaykh Mohammad Ali Shomali

AL-BURĀQ

Heighten The Mind

Copyright

ISBN: 978-1-956276-16-9
Printed and published by al-Burāq Publications.

Ordering Information
We offer discounts and promotions for wholesale purchases, non-profit organizations, and other educational institutions. Contact us at the email below for further information.

www.al-Buraq.org
publications@al-Buraq.org

First Edition | January 2020
Second Edition | April 2022

Dedication

The publication of this book was made possible
through the generous support of our donors.

Please recite *Sūrah al-Fātiha* and ask Allāh
for the Divine reward (*thawāb*) to be
conferred upon the donors and also the
souls of all the deceased in whose memory
their loved ones have contributed
graciously towards the publication of *Self-
Knowledge*.

Duaa al-Hujja

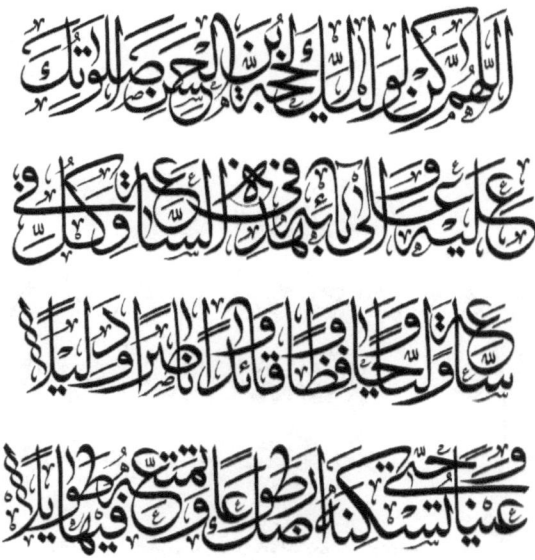

O Allah, be, for Your representative, the Hujjat (proof), son of al-Hasan, Your blessings be upon him and his forefathers, in this hour and in every hour: a guardian, a protector, a leader, a helper, a proof, and an eye - until You make him live on the Earth, in obedience (to You), and cause him to live in it for a long time.

Table of Contents

The Importance of Self-Knowledge

When discussing a topic such as this, it is perhaps best to begin with its definition and an assessment of its importance. Let us then begin by defining some terms. In Arabic self-knowledge is called Marafatul-Nafs. What is Marafatul-Nafs or self-knowledge? It is knowledge about us, but what kind of knowledge? It is not the kind that has to do with knowing one's name, or father's name, or the place and date of one's birth. Self-knowledge deals with another aspect of our being. It is not related to our physical senses, rather it deals with the spiritual dimension of our lives.

When we speak of the different dimensions of the spirit, and of our being, we should not forget that the human being is fundamentally different from other beings. Although we are anchored to the animal world in many ways, here we wish to focus on that which separates us from animals and is not found in them.

To understand better why this topic is of such importance, perhaps it helps to quote a few verses of the Glorious Qur'an and Hadiths on the subject. There are many verses in the Glorious Qur'an which elaborate. One of these verses is found in Surah al-Hashr, where the Almighty Allah says:

'And be not like those who forgot Allah, so He made them forget their own souls; these it is that are the transgressors."
(59:19)

Here the Lord is saying that forgetting Him causes us to forget ourselves in turn, and ultimately leads us to transgression.

There is a tradition that makes a similar point to that of this verse, but looks at the matter from another angle. This tradition is a very famous one, and it is difficult to find a book on ethics, which has not quoted it: "He who truly knows himself has known his Lord."

This tradition implies that self-knowledge implies knowledge about the Lord as well. Awareness of oneself leads to awareness of the Lord. And likewise, one who is oblivious of the Lord is oblivious of him. If one is determined to learn about one's Lord, then the best way to accomplish the task is to learn about oneself.

Another verse dealing with the topic is found in Surah al-Ma'idah, where Allah says:

"O you who believe! Take care of yourselves; he who errs cannot hurt you when you are on the right path." (5:105)

In this verse Allah is telling us to take care of ourselves, to pay attention to ourselves, that we must be careful about the well-being of our spirits, that we must be aware of the diseases of our souls, and how to cure them. He also tells us that we should pay attention to our duties, made obligatory on us as Muslims. Then He tells us that if we understand the way, that if we are faithful and committed believers, those who are misled will not harm us. From this we understand that our first duty is to take care of ourselves spiritually.

Sometimes a question may arise here about the relationship between the believer and society. Does the above verse mean that we should focus on ourselves and not pay any attention to the society at large? To answer this question let us see what Allamah Tabataba'i says on this topic in his landmark work, Al-Mizan.

This great interpreter and scholar of the Glorious Qur'an explains that what is meant here is that we should take care of ourselves, and be familiar with our social and private duties, so that we can also be socially responsible. For instance, in Islam we are commanded to advise people to do good and forbid them from evil deeds. One who does not perform this duty is not considered a devout Muslim, the reason being that he is not helping the society to better itself.

So, in Islam taking care of oneself spiritually is closely interwoven with being concerned with the welfare of the society as well. Conversely, it is important to remember that the society can greatly influence a person, weakening or strengthening one's faith.

Another question that may come up is "Are we responsible for guiding non-Muslims as well?" The answer is an unequivocal yes, although the most important thing before doing that is to conduct oneself in such a pious, righteous manner that others are able to see the immense practical benefits of being a faithful Muslim. In inviting non-Muslims to Islam, we are continuing the job entrusted to the noble Prophet (S) in his lifetime. It is also a duty demanded by our love for our fellow human beings. It we have found the way and the light, we should invite others to immerse themselves in the light and its blessings as well.

After performing our personal and social duties, those who are still disbelieving and those who still insist on erring, will not be harmful to us. Perhaps they will bother you, and at most they may kill you, but they will not be able to take your faith away from you. On the contrary, these pressures strengthen your faith.

Returning to our main theme, the third verse on the importance of self-knowledge is found in:

"We will soon show them our signs in the universe and in their own souls, until it becomes quite clear to them that ft is the Truth." (41:53)

Allah says that very soon we will show them our signs, but what are these signs and where will they be found? Allah tells us that these signs are found in two places: meaning in the external world and in their own souls. This ayah tells us that by considering these signs which are within our own selves and which are in the universe, it will become completely clear that Allah truly exists. According to some interpretations this fact will not only be true, but will be the truth itself. It is important to understand the distinction between these two expressions; it is the same when we say that Imam All (A.S.) is not only just but that he is just meaning that justice was embodied in Imam Ali (AS.).

Let us continue exploring the reasons the topic is so vital to our conduct in life. Once again we shall rely on the Glorious Qur'an for guidance. In everyday life when we purchase a new appliance or a gadget, we immediately turn to its manual for guidance in correctly operating it, believing that its manufacturer is the best source of guidance. So it seems quite logical for a Muslim to turn to the Glorious Qur'an for instructions on correct conduct in life, convinced that the Maker and Creator of human beings is also the best source of guidance in learning about the immensely complex nature of human beings.

Another verse pertaining to our topic is found in Surah al-Dhariydt:

'And there are signs on the earth for those who are certain. And in your own souls (too); will you not then see?" (51: 20, 21)

We learned that Allah has two kinds of signs, the ones in the external, physical world, and those within ourselves.

Verse 20 deals with those signs that have to do with the physical realm. In it the Almighty God tells us that there are signs on the earth for those who believe.

Immediately a question arises: why should those who already believe need the reassurances of such signs, and why should those who are not believers in God remain oblivious of them, yet more in need of them?

The answer given by great scholars of Islam is that those who do not believe in a creator as the Lord and Sovereign of the universe, also tend not to look or pay attention to that which is before them remaining for the most part oblivious of signs which are readily discernible to believers.

In the following verse, 21 of Surah al-Dhaaniitt, the Lord says:

"And in your own souls (too); will you not then see?"

This verse calls to our attention to the need to look for these signs within ourselves. We are clearly and unambiguously told that there are signs in the external world as well, and these are sources of guidance for us.

From these verses it becomes clear to us that Muslims are urged not to focus on their souls to the exclusion of the physical, material world; and conversely, not to think that material affairs are all that matter.

In India for instance, there are people who try to strengthen the power of their souls in order to enable themselves to perform certain deeds not ordinarily possible. But in so doing, they loose touch with the everyday life of the planet. That is not what faithful Muslims are commanded to do. Muslims are told the two go hand in hand and are complimentary to each other.

When a scientist is working on a project in the laboratory, or a person is performing the most menial of tasks to earn an honourable living, he or she is carrying out one of God's commandments. It is again, one of the most distinct characteristics of Islam that two worlds are never separated.

In today's world, in Western societies in particular, we see countless examples of people who are totally alienated from themselves, seeking all in the material life.

In more extreme cases, the alienation from the self has progressed to such a degree that being alone becomes painful and undesirable. Why? Because when such a person is alone, in a way he has lost contact with the eternal world, which is all he has. So being alone with his soul and spirit, he has to face a world which has no meaning to him, and matters not to him. In trying to escape the inevitable loneliness, many resort to mind-altering drugs, such as alcohol and narcotics.

A person with a healthy spirit can be alone yet not lonely. One who has forsaken a part of himself, his spirit, his consciousness, when alone, seeks to destroy it, rather than facing that which is excruciatingly painful; thus resorting to drugs becomes an easy escape route.

This is one reason why some societies use solitary confinement as a method of punishment for hardened criminals who already are serving life sentences and have nothing to lose by further acts of violence.

But when a faithful Muslim is alone by himself, he is not lonely. As a matter of fact being alone is prized by faithful Muslims. There is a Hadith from Imam Sajjad (A.S.) in which the Imam is quoted as saying: "If all between the East and West were to die, I would not feel lonely as long as the Qur'an was with me.

Once again we shall turn to the Hadiths to further explore this topic. This invaluable heritage has been left to us by the scholars who instinctively knew the eternal value of observing the speech and deeds of the Noble Prophet and Imams, and recording for posterity this living example of the perfect Muslim and human being.

Earlier we discussed a famous Tradition, which has reached us in two similar versions: There is however, no difference in meaning: "However knows himself (his soul or spirit) knows [or has known] his Lord "(1) Imam Ali (A.S.) is also quoted on the subject, stressing the importance of knowledge: "Knowledge of oneself (self-knowledge) is the most beneficial knowledge of all" (2)

This again tells us that knowing oneself leads to knowing one's Lord and all that it entails.

The second Hadith on the topic from Ali (A.S.) reads: "I wonder at the person who urgently searches for that which he has lost, but he has lost his soul and is not searching for it."

The third Hadith from Imam Ali (A.S.) on Self-knowledge is: 'I wonder how a person who ignores himself can know his Lord.'

The fourth Hadith from Imam Ali (A.S.) is: "Whenever the knowledge of a man increases, his attention to his soul also increases and he tries his best to train, and purify' it."

Here is yet another Tradition on the subject from Imam Ali (AS.): "The ultimate knowledge of a man is to know himself."

The Benefits of Self-Knowledge

One of the practical benefits of self-knowledge is to allow a person to become intimately familiar with his or her abilities and aptitudes. This is of immense help to a person in life, preventing one, for instance, from selecting a field of study or job inherently unsuitable to one's God-given abilities.

It also is of great value to a person to comprehend that he is not, theologically speaking, and self-existent. This is important, since it helps a person to understand that no matter how powerful or high one's station in life is, there are numerous events in life over which one has no control.

Of even more importance is the spiritual value of self-knowledge, in that one who has self-knowledge is much less likely to indulge in arrogance, undue pride, and other such destructive behaviours. One who is closely in touch with his own self and his Lord, is also much better equipped to improve those aspects of himself which can be improved, and do indeed need improvement. One can better appraise one's weaknesses and strengths, and be grateful for one's blessings.

Self-knowledge is a highly effective system of self-improvement; one can even say that is in some ways similar to the "biofeedback" therapies many physicians in some Western Countries recommend to patients whose active participation in the healing process is needed, or to patients for whom modern medicine has not found a cure.

Another very important benefit of is that a faithful Muslim knows that he or she is an extremely precious creation of Allah, and does not see himself simply as yet another animal with some basic needs to satisfy and strive for. Here we are going to turn for a moment to a rather philosophical discussion to better understand this point.

Most people seem to instinctively realise that every being has a different level of perfection, closely matched to that being's inherent characteristics and purpose in the scheme of things in the universe. For instance, an ordinary shade tree which does not bear fruits compared with an apple tree which does the latter as well as the former, is considered of a lower status of perfection in the scheme of things. It is for this reason that an apple tree in an orchard, which grows enough leaves to provide ample shade but for some reason does not bear fruit, is most likely cut down and replaced with one that does. It has not lived up to its potential, its level of perfection. In other words, although the tree remains useful in many respects, it has failed in that aspect that distinguishes it from the less perfect trees which do not bear fruits.

The same analogy works when comparing humans and animals. If a human being does not exhibit characteristics which rise above those shared with animals, i.e., eating, drinking, seeking comfort, shelter, pleasure, and the continuation of the race, then that human being has not reached his or her full potential, or perfection.

To summarise this point, one can logically claim that the second most important benefit is recognition of these innate, exclusive characteristics, allowing one to see clearly what they are. Such a human being will not allow himself to be corrupted and brought down to the level of animals, having understood his status in the scheme of things, and in the eyes of his Lord. Whoever discovers his true value will not commit any sins. If we truly understand what a precious being we are, our indescribably high potential, and the heights to which we can soar, then we will not allow ourselves to be shackled by sin, and held down.

Speaking of human beings that have risen to the heights of perfection, let us now see what that man of God and His servant Imam Ali (A.S.), says on the subject. The following two Hadiths are taken from Nahjul-Balghah:

"Whoever views himself with respect views his desires with disdain."

In other words, the Imam is saying that once a person becomes aware of himself, understands how precious he or she is, and the worthy goals he can set for himself; his own desires appear light, Insignificant, and unworthy to him. Thus, fighting temptation becomes easier, and this is one of the benefits of self-knowledge.

The second Hadith is from the letter that Imam Ali sent his son, Imam Hasan (A.S.), advising him on matters important to him. The words are like precious jewels, and we, the ordinary Muslims are more in need of hearing and remembering such advice than the Imam, to whom the letter was addressed:

"Keep yourself above every low thing even though ft may take you to your desires, because what you will receive in return is nowhere near worth that which you will have to give of yourself Do not let anything enslave you, for Allah created you free. "

In the Glorious Qur'an we find verses which point to the people who are totally lost:

"Most assuredly man is in loss, except those who believe And do good, and enjoin each other to the truth and patience."
(103:1-3)

So, as we see in both the Glorious Qur'an and the Hadiths, great emphasis has been placed on the issue of self-knowledge and on the resultant freedom, which ensues. Since there are many good interpretations written on the Glorious Qur'an, here we will try to provide a careful examination of the words of Imam Ah (AS) on the subject as well.

In the second Tradition, we find the word meaning deeds that are inherently ugly and demeaning. The

Imam warns us of the grave danger of such deeds to one's soul, for they enslave the spirit and corrupt the soul. He warns us to be ever-vigilant against actions which, although pleasurable, comforting, or convenient are so demeaning that one loses much, much more spiritually than one gains in momentary pleasures or comforts.

In the last sentence of the second Hadith, the Imam tells his son and us that human freedom is such a precious, prized gift of the Almighty God, that any deed, however pleasurable or convenient, which leads to enslavement, is an extremely bad deal. The momentary pleasure passes and the grievous damage persists.

Now let us continue on to another major benefit of self-knowledge. Most people instinctively realise that there are two distinct features to their being: the material, worldly aspect, and the spiritual aspect. Most however, do not understand or believe that the latter is incomparably more important. But in Islam, spiritual affairs rule supreme. One can be an enormously productive member of the society in material terms, and yet be considered unworthy to be called a Muslim if one is corrupt; while the opposite is unthinkable in Islam. So it is no wonder that being aware of and guarding against diseases of the spirit is so stressed in Islam. This extends to all actions, however seemingly insignificant.

There is a pervasive misconception that some deeds do not adversely affect one's soul because they seem unimportant. But we are taught in Islam that every deed, every word one utters, has an effect on one's soul and spirit, reinforcing the faith and purifying the spirit, or undermining the faith and harming one's soul. Words spoken to guide a lost soul are valuable both to the speaker and to the person gone stray. They each benefit in different ways. So there must not be any doubt among faithful Muslims that in Islam, we are taught that every action, every word has consequences for our spiritual well-being, and must be not dismissed as insignificant and trivial.

When The Noble Prophet (S) sent Imam Ali (AS) to Yemen, he said: "O Ali! Do not fight with anyone until you invite him [to Islam] and I swear by Him that if Allah guides one person through you, it will be more precious than all over which the sun rises and sets."

To round up our discussion of this benefit, it may be said that we are clearly and unambiguously told that the most important dimension of our being is the soul, and our actions and thoughts directly affect this prized gift of God.

We might consider it a bit extreme when told that Islam also teaches us that thoughts also must be watched for their effect on the spirit. We are also taught that in most of the cases demeaning one's thoughts may be, so long as one does not act on them one is not severely taken to task by the Lord. But sinful deeds have roots in the spirit, Muslims are admonished against jurisprudence and for mere thoughts or narrowly defined one is not punished

In Islam the immensely complex nature and nurture beings is subjected to two rather distinct set of rules: Fiqh, Islamic jurisprudence; Akhlaq ethics.

The obligatory rules of Fiqh are concerned with the minimally necessary conditions of human perfection. For humans aspiring to new heights, higher levels of perfection, Divine guidance is provided in the second set of rules, Akhlaq which governs both the world and the soul and provides us with all the Prescriptions we need to reach the highest levels of perfection. Thus, the two sets of rules governing Muslims' lives, are each meant for a different purpose. For instance, while idle chatter is not prohibited it is considered a waste of precious time and not helpful to the spiritual development of the person, and thus prohibited.

Another example which helps to illuminate the difference better is the night prayers, which is highly recommended to all Muslims; and while not mandatory in fiqh, it is compulsory in akhlaq. The reason being that those aspiring to new heights, and striving for perfection, are expected to prepare and develop spiritually by performing certain tasks, such as rising in the majestic dark of the night to offer prayers to the Lord of the universe.

So Fiqh mainly comprises basic and necessary laws whose obedience IS required from all Muslims, and is considered the first step towards development To commit oneself to the laws of Fiqh is not a difficult undertaking, as Islam itself is not a difficult religion.

However, there always are individuals who observe the mandatory laws of fiqh, yet upon getting a glimpse of the Light, want nothing more than to fly to the Flame. For these enraptured souls, Islam has provided akhlaq. They then make mandatory upon themselves deeds which are highly recommended, or mustahab In addition to performing these recommended tasks, they obey other laws of Akhlaq, and make. unlawful upon themselves that which is not forbidden in Fiqh, yet somehow might be an obstacle on the way to the Light, to perfection.

Therefore there might be thoughts or spiritual qualities which are not directly forbidden in Fiqh, but prohibited in Akhlaq. One destructive thought or quality which is not forbidden in itself in Fiqh is jealousy, which is not a punishable offence in Islamic jurisprudence, nor are we taken to task for such thoughts in the Hereafter. Yet actions issuing from jealousy might be forbidden.

The Noble Prophet said: 'if you are pessimistic then do not let that keep you from continuing, and if you are suspicious about someone, do not judge on that basis, and if you are envious of someone, do not persecute him "

Jealousy has been called the prison of the soul, and such an impediment to one's spiritual development that there is no place for it in akhlaq. We also can find examples of thoughts being the subject of the both sets of rules governing the life of Muslims. One of these, considered one of the greatest sins which mostly manifests itself in one's thoughts, is despair of

God's help. There are many Hadiths regarding this subject and it is so grievous a sin that it is considered a form of or disbelief in God. There are several reasons for this; and just from a psychological point of view, such a person, so lost in sin and so despondent of ever being forgiven by the Lord, has no practical incentive either to save himself, or to save the society from his future misdeeds. This feeling of despair, we are taught in Islam, is worse than the sins themselves.

Even in mandatory, practical laws, fiqh, Muslims are explicitly forbidden from ever losing hope in God's forgiveness. We are told that such despondent thoughts are one of the most effective weapons of Satan, who will rejoice at the spectre of a lost soul, despondent of his Lord's mercy and forgiveness. Such people are told to truly and sincerely repent, amend for past deeds to the extent possible, and have faith that the Almighty God will forgive them.

Another great sin, which also has to do mostly with one's thought, is to think oneself free of the possibility that God will not exact punishment for one's misdeeds. To consider oneself the master schemer somehow able to get away with sin. In the Glorious Qur'an we find:

"They planned and Allah planned, and He is the best of Planners." (3:54)

So we are told not to think ourselves beyond God's justice, and not to scheme and deceive, for it is all in vain. One of the words used in this verse is (makr) which when used for man, means deception; but when used in connection with Almighty God connotes planning in an innocent, yet capable manner. An example of this is found in the account of the Quart's attempt on the Noble Prophet's life. They thought their plan carefully through, and in order to spread the blame and avoid the consequences, sent one man from each tribe to carry out the assassination. They were certain that this scheme would prevent the kin and followers of Muhammad (S) from declaring war on all tribes should the culprits be found. But by God's Grace, the Archangel Gabriel revealed their plans to the Prophet and Ali (AS) decided to occupy his bed, and the Prophet left town that night.

To conclude our discussion of this topic, the third major benefit Of self-knowledge taught in Islam is to know that the spiritual aspect of our being is the most important one, and our spirits are influenced not only by our deeds but also by our ideas. So we must be on guard with respect to our thoughts, and use our knowledge of ourselves to avoid the many pitfalls of the soul. The fourth benefit of self-knowledge is to understand that we were not created by chance. if we deeply contemplate our own selves, our being, we come to the inevitable conclusion that it is God who created all, and we could not have come into existence by ourselves or simply as a result of our parents' union, had it not been part of His Plan. Naturally man is always in search of a reason for his existence, his being, but through contemplating creation and the goals of creation, one realises that we are each unique, with a mission in life. We were not created by chance and in vain.

Armed with this knowledge, one is well equipped to strive and to realise the purpose of one's creation, to incessantly seek to return to Him through deeds which are dear to him, Godly acts which are the cornerstone of religion and give life meaning. The fifth benefit is the tremendous help one receives in truly appreciating the element of consciousness, which is critical to the process of spiritual development and purification. Through self-knowledge, we are able to cultivate and develop our self-awareness, our consciousness; otherwise external factors may come to influence us in ways we cannot control.

One of the characteristics of man is that with respect to changing matters and constant ones, he is not always aware of the latter. This is so that our attention is not fixed and held on constants and we are therefore able to take measure of new things. Allah has made us in this way to enable us to attend to new matters; otherwise our attention would be fixed on only one thing. (Of course, it is possible for us to strengthen our spirit to pay close attention to more than one thing at the same time.) For example when we first put on a watch we are aware of it, but after a while we lose consciousness of it until we want to know the time; or we feel the weight of our clothes at first and then we neglect it. We feel hungry or not hungry through the changes of the size of our stomach.

We should utilise this psychological point in our spiritual lives. There are times when major catastrophes can befall one's soul, without the person being aware of it. There are instances of people who are totally lost in life and not even aware of the fact. This can progress to the extent of total disbelief in God, without the person being aware of the change in himself, in his consciousness. This is because humans are created in such a way that they are much more aware of sudden changes than subtle ones. One could undergo drastic changes in beliefs and yet these changes not be readily obvious to the person. A good example is lying. Most humans, specially in the early stages of childhood, cannot tell a lie, especially if it is the very first time they have engaged in such behaviour, without feeling uneasy, uncomfortable, and later, remorseful. As one repeats this behaviour though, the soul becomes inured to the effects, and one can lie, cheat, and deceive with little effort or discomfort. Even worse, one may not at all be conscious of the change one has gone through. Self-knowledge lets one see these changes coming, giving the person the opportunity to correct such character defects, and once again tread the path of God.

With most people however, only cataclysmic events in their personal lives can cause them to become aware of these character defects. With those armed with it will not come to that. By paying attention to one's consciousness and caring for it, one can gain awareness of the subtle changes that occur in the inner life and take corrective steps when needed.

The Almighty God tells us in the Glorious Qur'an:

"Then it was the fate (end) of those who did evil, to reject Divine signs, and become accustomed to mocking them."
(30:10)

So it is with human beings, given consciousness and free will, we can destroy ourselves or we (:an attain happiness and peace if we are aware of ourselves, our actions, and most importantly aware of the Almighty God at all times.

The sixth benefit of self-knowledge is that it serves as a gateway to the non-material or spiritual world. Once we pass through the gates we find many things which from a strictly materialistic point of view do not make sense. An example of this is the conscience, which can not be justified or explained by merely materialistic laws. I-low wonderful it is that all human beings from time immemorial, regardless of up-bringing, culture, and religion hear the same call from within. People seem to instinctively realise what is right and what constitutes a wrong. Every person considers oppression and injustice as bad, and justice as good and desirable. Even oppressors themselves wish to be treated justly. It is said that even thieves, when dividing the loot, pick the one among them they deem trustworthy to do the job.

Through self-knowledge we come to understand that all things except human beings have an inherent nature which cannot be changed. For instance, a stone is forever stone, no matter how many changes it goes though when different things are made of it. With human beings it is the exact opposite. Although we all inhabit more or less the same kind of a physical body, we have different natures. We are told that on the Day of Judgement, when the veil is finally lifted from before our eyes, we will see ourselves and others as they really are. Their true natures will appear. In the Glorious Qur'an we read:

"On the day when hidden things will be made manifest."
(86:9)

And there is another verse:

"The day on which the trumpet shall be sounded so you shall come forth in hosts." (78:18)

According to Hadith, hosts means groups of people and other beings, grouped according to their true natures. Some might appear as dogs or monkeys. Some human beings could have fallen lower than a bug, while others could have ascended higher than angels. We learned that in Islam, human beings are not valued the same. One can, through despicable deeds rank below the lowliest of species and conversely, rise higher than angels, in the eyes of God.

According to other worldviews, all human beings are considered as one and the same. Zionists and their victims, or Serbs and their victims are considered as humans with the same rights and both have to be respected. But in Islam, there are two distinct levels of humanity, therefore two distinct levels of laws, relationships, etc.

First, there are basic laws applied to all human beings, arising from their basic rights, their birth right for having been created human. The second level of laws are exclusively applied to real human beings, who through countless Godly deeds have risen to a level inaccessible to others who have not conducted themselves in a a similar fashion. The underlying reason for this is that the relationship between the Creator and man is a very special one, with the Lord granting certain rights exclusively to those who tread His path.

One aspect of this relationship, aside from the laws, is the insight that the Almighty God grants the faithful, enabling them to understand people's true natures and characters in this life. There are also some awesome privileges granted to the righteous which have not even been granted to angels. Again, the reason seems to be that man, given free will, when exceedingly righteous and pious, is also accorded certain privileges denied to angels. For instance, when the Noble Prophet ascended to the Heavens in the majestic night of Miraj (Ascension), he was at times accompanied by the Archangel Gabriel; but there were places and dimensions of the universe which were denied the archangel, for, in his words, quoted by the Noble Prophet: "If I had gone even a fingertip further I would have been burnt. "

In the Glorious Qur'an we read that when the Noble Prophet ascended to the Heavens he got as close as any created being could ever hope to the Lord of the universe:

"Then he drew near, then he hewed, so he was the measure of two bows or closer still. And He revealed to His servant what He revealed." (53: 8-10)

Here we should not forget that in the Glorious Qur'an at times the Lord speaks to us in allegory, especially when matters are well over our heads. So the distance mentioned here should also be taken in the same vein, meaning that the Noble Prophet was only two stages beyond seeing the Lord of the universe in all His Majesty.

These and matters like them are learned through It is, as mentioned earlier, the gateway to the non-material, metaphysical world. Thus, we reviewed some Islamic teachings regarding the widely divergent values of different human beings to their Creator and to each other. We also saw how self-knowledge helps open the Sates of the spiritual world, presenting a breathtaking vista to those who step inside.

As for those who choose a different life, sinking deep, and drowning in the vortex of sin, the Glorious Qur'an says:

"And certainly we have created for Hell many of the Jinn(I) and the men; they have hearts with which they do not

understand, they have eyes with which they do not see, and they have ears with which they do not hear; they are as cattle, nay, they are in worse error, they are the heedless ones."
(7:179)

These, who remain totally oblivious of their Lord and the spiritual aspects of themselves, are called "dead," by the Glorious Qur'an Since we are taught that of the two aspects of our live, the physical, material life and the spiritual life, the latter is much, much superior, and is centred on faith and deed. To be truly alive and aware in this world, we are taught in the Glorious Qur'an to believe in the Almighty God, His words, and His last Prophet:

"O' believers! Accept the words of Allah and the Prophet when he calls you to that which gives you life." (8:24)

Some people only have the physical life, and therefore can comprehend only material, physical things; others have both the physical and spiritual lives, thus can understand both. Given the immensely constructive role religion as a framework for conduct in this life can play in people's lives, and the overall world view which it presents to the faithful to guide their lives, it is astounding that today a great number of people forsake their faiths. To some this is because they feel they will lose their "freedom" to do as they wish, that religion somehow takes away their freedom, and one would be a slave, so to speak. Well, we are all slaves, in a way. Some of God, some of money, power, desires, etc. The way then to be truly free is to obey God and His Commandments, and release oneself from other "gods". It is not an easy task satisfying many gods, but to please one, especially when the belief itself strengthens the person, and releases one from limitations, is not a difficult undertaking.

The person who chooses God, is no longer a slave of others, but has reached a level of lordship. We see in Hadiths that: "The servant-ship is a substance whose essence is the lordship. "

The Prophet of Islam was a slave of the Almighty God by choice. We also express this sentiment several times a day during our ritual prayers: "I bear witness that Muhammad is His servant and Messenger."

Yet this seemingly bonded man changed the history of the world. He successfully fought powers which opposed God, yet was honoured to prostrate himself before Allah. Anything but freedom is one's reward when one selects a life without religion, without a relationship with the Creator.

"Have you seen him who takes his low desires for a god? Will you then be a protector over him? Or do you think that most of them do hear or understand? They are nothing, but cattle, nay, they are straying further of the Path." (25:43-44)

"Allah sets forth an example: There is a slave in whom are (several) partners differing with one another, and there is another slave wholly owned by one man. Are the two alike in condition? (All) praise is due to Allah. Nay most of them do not know." (39:29)

There are three couplets attributed to Imam Ali (AS) with which we will end our discussion. It only seems fitting, since the Imam's words eloquently show the importance of self-knowledge: "The cure is with you, but you do not see, And the illness is from you, bur you are unaware. You are the clear book whose letters make manifest the hidden. Do you think you are some small mass while within you there dwells a great world?"

Free Will

In previous discussions we studied the status of human beings in the Glorious Qur'an. We saw that they are not at the same level. They can be higher than angels and they can be representatives (caliphs) of Allah on earth. They can also go downwards and be lower than animals. It is up to human beings themselves to select their own way of life.

In this part we want to study free will and answer those who believe in determinism. If someone believes in determinism he will lose his hope in a better future and will not try to purify himself. Some criminals or despotic rulers used to justify their crimes and sins by saying that they were determined. So it is necessary to refute determinism as one of the most dangerous obstacles against purity of the soul.

The next step will be to see how we select something and what we should select and what we should observe in our selection or decision. The question that arises is: "Are human beings free to do what the person (or even independent being). Having understood the non-existence of the society, it is obvious that there is no place to claim that some demands of the society determine the behaviour of its members.

Individuals are makers of societies through their free will, just as they make history. It is noteworthy that these individuals are not separated from each other. There is a close relationship between them. There is a strong interaction among them. So if someone wants to adapt his actions and activities to social ideals it will be very easy for him because other members of the society or at least the majority agree with him and they will support him. But if someone wants to change his society, it needs many efforts, constant work. Even if someone wants to conduct his life in his own way, in spite of others, it will be very difficult, for there are many interactions between individuals in the society. To be religious in a religious society is much easier than in a non-religious society, but it is not necessary. Also, to be a real Muslim in some society which is not committed to Divine morals and values is difficult, but it is not impossible.

According to Islam every person is responsible]e for his actions. On the Day of Judgement no one can say that he was bad because he lived in a bad family or society. But on the other hand all people are responsible for their societies. No one can say that he had nothing to do with his society. If children are being attracted by enemies or some Muslim youth are imitating Western habits or generally a Western way of life and I can do something about it with my thought or my money or so on, I cannot say: it is none of my business."

Natural Determinism:
Some people believe that according to the natural laws not only our body is formed and controlled by nature, but also our thoughts and behaviours are all controlled by nature or natural factors which are not decided or

planned by ourselves. These determinists emphasise the effects of climate, environment, food, medicine and inheritance. It is possible to make a person sad or happy with some~foods or medicine. If a person's father is an artist, a painter, that person will be an artist as well.

This view is partly true. Natural factors have some effects on our behaviour or actions, but they are not absolute. Finally it is up to a person to decide for himself. Those external factors might make the process of decision-making easier or harder. However, a human being is free. If a person's parents are illiterate, that person will not have to be the same. If the parents are bad, the possibility of him being good is not nil. As we see in history there existed good people amongst bad people and vice versa. Take the example of Noah's son. Although Noah (A.S.), the father, was a prophet of God, his son chose to become a bad and disobedient servant of God. When Noah made the ship and called all the people to board it, his son refused and claimed on the top of a mountain thinking the water would not reach him. Allah says:

'And Noah called out to his son, and he was aloof O my son! Embark with us and be not with the unbeliever He said: I will betake myself if for refuge to a mountain that shall protect me from the water Noah said: There is no protector today from Allah's punishment except for whom He has mercy; and a wave intervened between them, so he was of the drowned." (11:42-43)

Thus, Islam pays attention to the children's upbringing and training before, during and after birth. All these are taken into account, but their influences are not decisive as free will is preserved.

Religious Determinism:

There are some sects in Islam and other religions which believe that Allah decides for us and none of us is free to do what he wants.

This belief is mainly due to lack of knowledge. For instance, they say whether a person prays or not, whether he is truthful or not, whether he is an oppressor or not, is all because of Allah's will and human beings have no say or fault in this matter.

This belief was developed by some theists to preserve monotheism. They thought that if we say people are free in their life, it means that Allah has nothing to do in this part of the world and it is up to human beings to do whatever view monotheism demands the denial of any human role in action. They also misunderstood some verses of the Glorious Qur'an.

This view is completely against Divine justice. It is also against Divine wisdom (hikmah). According to this view sending prophets and inviting people to the religion and Divine commands are useless. If this view were true, then Allah would not have assigned rewards and punishments for our actions.

The evil intentions and politics of some despotic rulers like the Umayyads and Abbasids is another reason for the appearance of this belief in Islamic culture. They spread this belief for their own desires and benefits. They said that Allah had given power to them and no one was able to interfere in His deeds. So no one was allowed to protest against them. If the Ahlul-bayt (people of the household of the Prophet) were not allowed to rule, it was because Allah wanted this, or if Yazid as a ruler did many bad things nobody had a right to say anything. For example, when Imam Husain was martyred, 'Ubayd Allah, the son of Marjanah and the commander of Kufa, took members of the Ahl al-bayt as prisoners.

He said in the great mosque of Kufa: "Praise be to Allah Who has made righteousness successful and has helped the leader of the believers (meaning Yazid) and his followers and killed the liar, the son of the liar." When he took the prisoners to his palace, he addressed Zaynab (AS) and said: "Praise be to Allah Who destroyed your respect and killed you and proved that you are liars." Then Zaynab (AS) spoke and defeated him. Then he turned his face to Imam Sajjad, the fourth Imam (AS), and asked who he was. Some answered: "Ali, the son of Husain."

He said: "Did Allah not kill Ali, the son of Husain?" Imam said: "I had a brother who was also called Ali, the son of Husain. People killed him." Then 'Ubayd Allah' said: "No, Allah killed him." When Imam disproved his claim he became very angry and commanded his soldiers to cut Imam's neck off, but Zaynab said:

"O son of Ziyad! You did not leave any of our men alive. If you want to kill him, You must kill me with him"

These rulers tried to attribute everything to Allah in a wrong way to conceal their role. There were also some weak and ignorant Muslims who wanted to justify their weak and bad behaviour through determinism and attributing everything to Allah. Praise be to Allah we have today pure Islam and we can easily solve the problem. We know that monotheism does not demand determinism at all.

Now let us quote some Qur'anic verses on this topic.

"Say O Allah, Master of the kingdom! Thou givest the kingdom to whomsoever Thou pleases and takest away the kingdom from whomsoever Thou pleases, and Thou exalts whom Thou pleasest and abases whom Thou pleasest; in Thine hand is the good; surely, Thou hast power over all things." (3:26)

This verse has one of the pictures that show monotheism (tawi}rd) very well and it is a must for every Muslim to believe in monotheism in this way (mentioned in the verse). Some people misunderstand or misuse this verse. They say that according to this verse, Allah had given the power of rulership to all despotic rulers. We should know that Allah has two kinds of will (iradah):

Generative: This kind of will is necessary in every thing. If there is something or there is not, it is because of Allah's will. Nothing in the universe is independent from Allah, the Creator. For example, if the weather is hot it is because of Allah's will or if I am alive it is because Allah wants. Every single action in this world is done because of His will. Does this mean Allah is satisfied with all the actions of human beings? No, although Allah's will is in their actions, He has given them free will at the same time to choose the right way. Here comes the second type of Divine will.

Legislative: This is about goodness and badness, about what to do and what not to do. He commands to do good and refrain from bad. So all good actions are done according to this will and all bad actions are done against this will. In order to make this conception clear, let us take the example of Imam Husain (A.S.). Was he killed through Allah's will? The answer is "Yes" and "No": Yes according to the generative will and No according to the legislative will.

As far as the generative will is concerned, nothing can be done without Allah's will. But this does not mean that He is pleased with all actions. This is the point of misunderstanding which leads to determinism. Another example: One father gives some money to his son to buy something and advises him to buy good things like books. The son is not determined to buy. Whatever he buys is according to his father's decision, but if he buys cigarettes he buys against Ms father's advice. No one can say that this son was independent in his action and also no one can say that this son had to buy cigarettes or he was not responsible arguing from the fact that his father made him able to do that.

Thus, the above verse (3:26) talks about His generative will. It does not mean that Allah is pleased with rulers like Pharaoh or Yazid. Another verse is the following verse which expresses the idea of free will explicitly.

"Surely we have created man from a small life-germ uniting (itself): We mean to try him so We have made him hearing, seeing. Surely We have shown him the way: he may be thankful or unthankful." (76-2,3)

So Allah has shown us the way. It is in our hand to be thankful or not. How can we be thankful? By using His blessings in the right manner and not only by saying thanks be to God. Another verse:

"It is naught but a reminder for the nations, for him among you who pleases to go straight And you donor will, unless God wills, the Lord of all Being." (81:27-29)

Thus the Glorious Qur'an is useful for those who want to go straight. They are free. They just have to take the first step and Allah will help them. But their decision is not independent of Allah's generative will (to enable them). They will what Allah wills. In the following verse again the doctrine of free will is expressed.

'Most surely there is a reminder in this for him who has a hean or he gives ear with a present mind." (50:37)

The process of being a faithful person is not a physical or chemical process, but a spiritual one. It does not need material things. It needs attention and consciousness.

Our Future

We mean by this title our situation after death. We can define death as the separation of the spirit from the body. Sleeping is to some extent like death. There is however a difference. During sleep the spirit is still connected with the body, but to a lesser degree than waking. But during the death the spirit is disconnected from the body and belongs to another body which has the qualities of a material body like shape and size without the mass. Philosophers compare it with the bodies of dreams. They call them 'barzakh' or 'mithalt'. This continues until the resurrection. Then our spirits will belong to another body which is like the body in its present situation. In this way we believe in the physical-spiritual resurrection.

This topic is very controversial. Even those people who believe in the physical-spiritual resurrection have reached no consensus about the nature of the bodies in that universe. But what we have said can be easily understood from the Glorious Qur'an and Islamic traditions on which great Islamic scholars agree, and this suffices us in our discussion. As we know, the most important part of our being which makes our personality is. the spirit. All rewards and punishments are in one way or another related to the spirit. The body is just a means for the spirit. Note the following two verses of the Glorious Qur'an.

'Allah takes the souls at the time of their death, and those that die not during their sleep; then He withholds those on

whom He has passed the decree of death and sends the others back till an appointed term." (39:42)

These verses show that death is not an end of our being, that during death our spirits will be completely received by Allah or according to the other verse we will be completely received by and that sleeping is to some extent like death. These verses answer many questions about the resurrection, but they are not closely related to our discussion.

Heaven and Hell

There are many facts about heaven and hell. We try to explain only those facts which help us in our project. Heaven and hell have been created now. If we had purified ourselves, we would be able to see them. Imam Ali says about the pious: "To them paradise is as though they have seen it and are enjoying its favours. To them hell is also as if they have seen it and are suffering punishment in it.

The Glorious Qur'an also speaks about hell:

"Nay! If you had known with a certain knowledge you should most certainly have seen hell." (102:5,6)

In this way we can say that our future is now present. Whoever is good, is now in heaven and criminals or sinners are now in hell. I hope the reader remembers that the companion of the Noble Prophet (S) who reached certainty said that he could declare among those who were with the Prophet who were people of hell and who were people of heaven. The Prophet (S) has also said that during the ascension, 'miraj' he saw workers (angels) planting trees. Sometimes they were working and sometimes they stopped working. Then he was told that when a person recites certain invocations of God a tree is planted for him and when he stops no tree is planted for him. This tradition like many other traditions shows that punishments and rewards are synchronous with the actions.

Three kinds of relationships can be conceived between acts and rewards or punishments:

Conventional relationship: Ordinary rewards or punishments are decided (defined) by some law-refiners. So they vary in different societies. For example, penalties for breaking traffic laws are from this kind.

Causal relationship: Sometimes rewards or punishments are effects of the acts. For example, when a person drinks wine, one of his punishments is loss of his health; or if a student studies well one of his rewards is to learn his lessons. The loss of health and knowledge are effects brought into being by those acts.

Unity: Sometimes rewards or punishments are nothing other than the actions. They are just the realities of those actions made manifest in another universe.

According to the Glorious Qur'an in the Hereafter the realities of the acts will be seen. This is what we mean by the embodiment of deeds (tajassum al-a 'mat):

"On that day men shall come forth in sundry bodies that they may be shown their works. So he who has done an atom's weight of good shall see it And he who has done an atom's weight of evil shall see it." (99:8)

"(As for) those who swallow the property of the orphans unjustly, surely they only swallow fire into their bellies and they shall enter burning fire." (4:10)

According to these and some other verses we will see our acts themselves. if we had that sight today we would be able to see their realities today. Whoever is swallowing the property of the orphans unjustly is really swallowing fire now. Whoever is back-biting is really eating the flesh of his dead brother or sister now. So we should take care of our acts, otherwise we will enter hell just now (not only in the future). if we think constantly about the ugliness of the sins and their realities we will not commit any sin.

Endless future

Every person lives in this universe for a limited time. Death is the unquestionable end for this life. Nothing can save men from death:

"Wherever you are, death will overtake you, though you are in lofty towers." (4:78)

After Barzakh those who enter heaven will be there forever:

"Those who are in awe of the Beneficent God in secret and come with a penitent heart: Enter it in peace, that is the day of abiding." (50:33, 34)

Those people who enter bell are of two kinds. Disbeliveers who are against the truth will stay there forever. But those believers who will enter hell for their bad deeds will finally enter heaven after they will have been cleansed.

"So as to those who are unhappy, they shall be in the fire; for them shall be sighing and groaning in it, abiding therein so long as the heavens and the earth endure, except as your Lord please; surely your Lord is the mighty doer of what He intends. And as to those who are made happy, they shall be in the garden, abiding in it as long as the heavens and the earth endure, except as your Lord please; which shall never be cut off." (11:106-108)

'And (as to) those who disbelieve, their guardians are Shaytans who take them out of the light into the darkness; they are the inmates of the fire, in it they shall abide."
(2:257)

Infinite rewards or punishments

A group of people will enter heaven and stay there forever. This entrance might be immediately after the judgement or after some interval. The other group will enter hell and stay there forever. So in respect to time there is no limitation. There is also no limitation in respect to the intention (the quantity and the quality). We cannot campare His rewards with the pleasurable things in this universe. According to the Glorious Qur'an there is whatever they like in heaven.

"Therein shall be what their souls yearn after and (wherein) the eyes shall delight." (43:71)

"They have therein what they wish and with Us is more yet." (50:35)

Not only they can get and enjoy whatever they want, but also there are things which they were not able to conceive. We usually wish what we have seen or generally experienced in advance. For example, people like to have a big house (with a big garden in a size and with qualities which cannot be found in this world). But there are still some blessings in heaven which are not familiar to men so they will receive them without any previous want or request.

"So no soul knows what is hidden for them of that which will refresh the eyes; a reward for what they did." (32:17)

According to traditions there is in Paradise what no eye has seen and no ear has heard and no heart has conceived (imagined). We cannot understand the torments either. The fire there is not comparable with ordinary fires. That fire burns the spirit as well as the body.

"And what will make you realise what the crushing disaster is? It is the fire kindled by Allah, which rises above the hearts. Surely it shall be closed over upon them in extended columns." (104:5-9)

Those who enter hell and suffer its torments wish to die. They think in this way they can get rid of the torments.

'And they shall call out O Mahk Let your Lord make an end of us. He shall say: Surely you shall tarry." (43:77)

"Then therein he shall neither live nor die." (87:13)

Whenever the fire bums their skin, Allah renews their skin to suffer again:

"So often as their skins are thoroughly burned, We will change them for other skins." (4:56)

Listen to Imam Ali (AS) in his prayer when he says: "O My Lord! And You know that I cannot endure the tribulations and punishments of this world and whatever ordeals happen to its inhabitants, while they are not so difficult and so long. So how can I endure the tribulations of the Hereafter and its great ordeals, while they are very long in their time and endless and their sufferers are not given any respite, because they are from of Your anger and vengeance and discontent and These cannot be withstood by the heavens and the earth.

Good Attributes of Human Beings

There are many attributes of human beings and many verses about them. We present the most important ones. The human being is the vicegerent on this earth:

'And when your Lord said to the angels: I am going to place on the earth a vicegerent." (2:30)

'And He it is who has made you successors in the land and raised some of you above others by (various) grades, that He might try you by what He has given you." (6: 165)

Humans have the greatest capacity for knowledge:

"And He taught Adam all the names, then presented them to the angels; then He said: Tell me the names of those if you are right." (2:31)

"Names" in the preceding verse means "realities". When angels thought that they were superior to Adam, Allah, the Most Glorious, wanted to prove that the angels were wrong. The Almighty taught Adam all the facts, and then asked the angels if they were true in their claim, then they would have to divulge those facts to Him. But they were not able to do so. Thus, we can understand from this verse that man is capable of attaining all knowledge.

Human beings are created in such a way that they can know their Creator through innate knowledge. Man has no need to use external ways for knowing Allah. If we go deep into our spirits we can understand that we are created, that we have a Lord. To illustrate an example, a person went to Imam Ja'far alSadiq (AS) and asked him to prove the existence of Allah, the Most Glorious. The Imam (AS) asked him whether he ever travelled on a ship. The man answered positively. Then the Imam (AS) asked him whether in his travel a situation arose where there existed a danger for the ship to sink and that people began to panic and were afraid that the ship would be wrecked and they would die as result. The man again gave an affirmative answer. The Imam (AS) then asked: "Did you think of any power that could have saved you then"? When the man said, "Yes," Imam concluded, "That is Allah, the Omnipotent".

When we are in danger and we feel no one can help us, inborn knowledge is awakened and activated. In many people and in ordinary situations, this knowledge of Allah the Most Glorious is dormant. However it can be awakened and strengthened, especially when we lose our shelter and strength and feel helpless. It is noteworthy that not only our knowledge of Allah is inadequate) but also the religion of Islam as a whole is in accordance with our spirit. And this is one of the key factors in its survival under very trying conditions and its extraordinary development. The following verse shows this fact.

"Then set your face upright for the religion in the right state the nature made by Allah in which He has made men; there is no altering of Allah's creation; that is the right religion, but most people do not know." (30:30)

Almighty Allah has created man in a manner that he becomes aware of the right religion and has strong affinity towards it. These are two dimensions of fitrat (the manner of our creation). We will not discuss fitrat in detail, but here it is necessary to say that this quality is the nature in man instilled by Allah.

The term fitrat means a God-given quality in all human beings. Innate matters are of two kinds: knowledge and desire. So, man's fi(n (natural) instinct consists partly of knowledge and partly of desire (natural drives). Therefore, we can say that every person through his innate God-given knowledge and desire is instinctively aware of the pure religion and has an affinity towards it.

However, when a person is immersed in material life and ordinary affairs and does not pay any attention to nonmaterial ideas, his fitrat (innate knowledge) and desire will become clouded. We know that proper nourishment is necessary for the growth of the body. If we neglect the right type of diet, it could lead to different kinds of complications that could cause a malfunction in the body. It is the same with fitrat. If we just indulge in material life, the other side will be weakened or clouded by material affairs. But in difficulties, when our attention to the material life is temporarily diverted, we turn entirely to Allah and slowly begin to feel the change from inside.

Besides the corporeal body, there is a Divine element or spiritual element in the human being. What does the Divine spirit mean? Does it mean that Allah has a spirit and has part of it in humans? Definitely not. When we attribute spirit to Allah, it is something symbolic, just like the House of Allah. Although every thing is created by Allah, some things are more precious and respected than others, so we attribute them to Allah.

Thus, we can conclude that all men have a Divine element in them, which is very important and which makes man a worthy being. The angels were commanded to prostrate before Adam (AS) only after Allah had breathed life into him-that is instilling the Divine Spirit into Adam. This spirit is the origin and the source of all special and exclusive perfection's of human beings. All the capabilities of this species originate from this endless and everlasting source-the Divine Spirit. Therefore, all of us are indebted to the Almighty, the Creator, for this irrecompensable Blessing.

Man was not created haphazardly through chance.

God has created human beings.

God has created human beings with a purpose. God has chosen human beings as his vicegerents.

These three facts prove that humans are chosen to be Allah's representative on this earth above all other creatures. We shall study how these three prominent factors are presented in the Glorious Qur'an.

"Then He made him complete and breathed into him of His spirit and made for you the ears and eyes and the hearts; little is it that you give thanks." (32:9)

As we stated in the previous chapter, man has been chosen by Almighty Allah, the Creator, as his vicegerent. The following is yet another verse confirming the basis of our discussion.

"Then his Lord chose him, so He turned to him and guided (him)." (20:122)

Some human beings are chosen by God. The phrase "turned to him" is tawbah in Arabic, which literally means to return. Sometimes it is attributed to God and sometimes to humans. When someone commits an error, God turns to him to help him. The Lord thus prepares the way for him to repent. And when he repents, and seeks forgiveness, God returns to him which means that God accepts his repentance. It is very clear that if God does not help us to return we cannot repent. God first helps us. He turns to man, then man repents and then God accepts his repentance. Notice the following verse:

"Then He turned to them (mercifully) that they might turn (to Him); surely Allah is the Oft-returning (to mercy), the Merciful." (9:118)

Man is completely free to chose his destiny. That is, man is the master of his own fate. This is how the Scripture presents the idea of one's destiny. There is the light of guidance. However, one is free to take it or:

"Surely we have shown him the way; he may be grateful or ungrateful" (76:3)

To be thankful does not mean to just say: "shukran lillah" (Thanks be to Allah). We should thank God for having given us to the righteous path and given us innumerable blessings without expecting anything from us. So, let's open our real eyes and see for ourselves His endless blessings. Being thankful to Him is not based on just mere utterances. We should try to use His blessings in such a way that we get closer to Him to further be blessed by the light of His Benevolence, Guidance and final reunion.

Both men and jinn have been bestowed the freedom to chose their ways and style of life. As we know, no other creatures have such a choice except the jinn's. The jinn have the freedom to believe or disbelieve. But the level of perfection jinn can reach is lower than that of men. Based on such principles jinn must follow the prophets who have been sent to the human masses.

Jinn like all human beings have all the biological functions. They reproduce like all living beings. However, their physical structure differs from that of man. Their bodies are light. They are not three dimensional. Jinn's can easily move about. They are able to move from one part of the universe to the other easily. Jinn's can take the forms of animals, humans, etc., but their creation lacks that ultimate potentiality of perfection with which mankind has been endowed.

Therefore, it is only humans who bear the Divine trust and fulfil the goal of creation: "We offered the trust to the heavens and the earth and the mountains, but they refused to carry it and were afraid of it; and man carried it. Surely he is very unjust, very ignorant." (33:72)

Man is respected and has honour:

'And surely We have honoured the children of Adam, and We have carried them in the land and the sea, and we have given them to excel by an appropriate excellence over most of those whom we have created." (17:70)

H. Human beings have a God-given power of judgement and discrimination, conscience.

Everyone understands what is good and what is bad. Prophets, thus, were sent to make people aware and strengthen their powers of understanding. For example, everyone is aware that to lie is wrong. Thus, the prophets came to emphasise the difference between right and wrong. They also teach us things which we were not aware of, such as details. This God-given power can be understood from the following verse:

"And the soul and Him who perfected it. Then He inspired it to understand what is right and wrong for it" (91:78)

Man's success depends on the soul. His discrimination of good from bad is not enough. He should act on the knowledge he has been given by Almighty Lord. Man will never be satisfied by anything except by the remembrance of Allah and drawing near to Him.

"Those who believe and whose hearts are set at rest by the remembrance of Allah; now surely by Allah's remembrance are the hearts set at rest" (13:28)

Every human being tries to reach his Lord. A person who wishes to acquire infinite wealth also tries to reach Allah, but his mistake is that he misunderstands his God. So he reaches for something insecure and transient. Every one wishes to reach Allah but man makes mistakes. The only way to fulfil oneself is by making one's soul aware of Allah. We should try to reach Him with full knowledge and be conscious of the goal we are trying to reach:

"O man! surely you strive (to attain) to your Lord, a hard striving until you meet Him." (84:6)

There are three types of souls. The highest is the confident soul, the most perfect soul that has obeyed Allah, to the extent that nothing can shake it, like Imam Husain's (A.S.) soul (as it is expressed in some aHadith). In order to attain this level, we must be in remembrance of Allah in each second of our worldly life. Every expression of our life, our ideas, thoughts, deeds, looks, actions, everything that one can imagine should express Him rather than us:

"O soul that is at rest. Return to your Lord, well pleased (with Him), well pleasing (Him)." (89:27, 28)

Having a confident heart depends on the remembrance of Allah, the Glorification of his Attributes of Beauty and Grandeur.

This is the secret key to our ascendance and the attainment of station or rank. One should try to ponder the attributes of His Beauty and Grandeur. Man will never be satisfied by anything except by the remembrance of Allah. These are great topics in Islamic thought.

Many problems in society can be resolved through money or material gain. But the innate problems of humanity cannot be solved by such things. Confidence is not gained by financial matters. Surely, this is not the case. We should ask ourselves this question: why do some of the richest people commit suicide? The fact is that these people initially thought that once they attained a status of wealth, they would have satisfied the ego. They would have a peaceful life. No sooner had they attained riches, than they began to realise that money alone cannot solve the problem. There was something missing in them.

The Divine blessings on earth are created for human beings who are free to utilise the land, harvest the seas, conquer space, utilise animals, etc. to their own benefits and ends.

'And He has made subservient to you whatsoever is in the heavens and whatsoever is on the earth, all, from Himself; most surely there are signs in this for a people who reflect."
(45:13)

"It is He who created for you all-that is in the earth." (2:29)

Man is created to worship Allah the Glorious:

'And I have not created the jinn and the men except to serve Me." (51:56)

This verse shows that one of the goals of our creation is to serve Allah the Exalted. We are not created merely to eat, drink, and sleep. The ultimate perfection of the human beings cannot be achieved except through the worship of Almighty Allah.

Man cannot know himself unless he knows Allah. A man cannot forget Allah, otherwise he will forget himself.

Why was man created?

What is his fate?

What should he do now?

These are some of the questions that can be un4erstood if mankind knows its Creator. Man will understand many realities after his death.

Men are mostly unaware of many things in this universe. They have limited knowledge and are only concerned with their day to day activate their daily routine. They care little of things beyond the material world. When death overtakes them, the curtains are parted. It is at that juncture that their eyes are opened to see the realities in their nakedness-everything uncovered. It is at this stage that they begin to perceive the Grandeur of the Creator, their misconceptions, their rejections, their negligence, their deeds whether good or bad. Before their eyes, they will see the angels, the burning inferno of hell for the bad deeds, and the everlasting bliss of Paradise for the good deeds.

Death awakens them to realise, possibly too late, that the Islamic ideas were the consummation of the heavenly religions dispensing truth in the fullest possible sense-the Words of Almighty Allah. They are then filled with fright and uncertainty of what they bad neglected. They are filled with remorse of the lost opportunity, which is impossible to compensate it is water under the bridge. If one tries to lessen his or her or her dependence on material life, be can reap the benefits in this very world. If money or fame is not important to one, but only remembrance of Allah and things concerning Allah, then one can see those realities which are hidden from others in this world.

"Certainly you were heedless of it, but now We have removed from your veil, so your sight today is sharp." (5: 22)

The Almighty Lord sent apostles, messengers, prophets and Imams to make us aware of both the spiritual and material aspects of life. Allah has never wanted us to be unconscious of the facts. Allah, the Creator wants us to be aware of the path we choose for this worldly and other worldly life.

The Lord wants us to enter another world with the bliss of soul and peace of mind. Almighty Allah sent His

Last Messenger, the Seal of the Prophets, Muhammad (S) to invite us to Islam, as the consummation of all the heavenly religions. So, it is in the interest and benefit of the human masses to follow and abide by Islamic law through which their eyes will be opened to the naked facts.

However, in general, it is unfortunate to see that people are in deep slumber in this material world but as soon as they pass to the next stage, the other world, they immediately become conscious of what is really going on(1) and return to this world is rendered impossible.

A verse in the Glorious Qur'an speaks of the unrighteous people. When they die they ask Allah:

"Until when death overtakes one of them, he says: Send me back, my Lord; Hapty I may do good in that which I have left. By no means! It is a (mere) word that he speaks; and before them is a barrier until the day they are raised" (23:99, 100)

Human beings usually becomes conscious only at the time of death. That is why we should read the Qur'an very carefully and when we reach these verses, we should stop and reflect on them. After death our sight will become more sharp and we will see and realise many things. But Imam Ali (AS) said in this regard: 'If the curtains are removed for the people, my certainty will not increase. '

He means that he has attained the depth of certainty which cannot be enhanced by any means. He has attained the station of Truth. Once the Prophet (S) was walking with some of his companions, and they met a young man whose strange behaviour attracted their attention.

The Prophet (S) asked him: "HOW are you?"

The young man replied: "I am certain."

The Prophet (S) said: "There is a sign for everything. If you have attained the rank of certainty, what is the sign for your certainty?"

The man replied: "My certainty tells me to fast in hot days and to pray all night. This is my sign. I have reached a stage that worshipping Allah alone is the only pleasure that I dearly derive. I see heaven and hell. And of those around you, I can see who are the people of heaven and of hell."

The Prophet (S) stopped him and said: "Say no more. Because it is not good to tell others of their future". The young man begged the Prophet (S) to pray to Allah to grant him the status of martyrdom. The Prophet (S) prayed, and later the man was martyred on a battlefield. That young man's good deed and his detachment from the material world earned him the status of having attained certainty. His soul was free and he could see what a person who has his heart set on the worldly glitters could not see. The Glorious Qur'an states that if we attained the status of certainty we could even see heaven and hell.

"Nay! if you had Known with a certain knowledge) You should most certainly have seen the hell." (102:5, 6)

Heaven and hell have been created for us, and they are not something that will be created in the future. A person who has pure insight can see them. Once a man named Rammam went to Imam Ali (A.S.) and asked him to tell him the qualities of the pious (muttaqrn) to the extent that he could see them. First Imam Ali (A.S.) did not want to say anything but Hammam insisted. One of the points mentioned by the Imam was that these people are like the people who have seen heaven and hell.

Men do not desire only material matters. People have some important things to consider as ideals. They can try their best only to attain the blessings and pleasures of Almighty Allah. The following verse explains that His pleasure is the most important reward.

"Allah has promised the believing man and believing woman gardens, beneath which rivers flow to abide in them, and goodly dwellings in gardens of perpetual abode; and best of all is Allah's goodly pleasure that is the grand achievement." (9:72)

This is the greatest achievement and not the material things. Here God explains the benefits and blessings in Paradise, and says that to be aware that God is satisfied with you, and that He is pleased with you, is the greatest blessing. This knowledge for man is extremely important. The desire of every person is to obtain the pleasure of Allah, the Glorious.

How to Reach Our Goal

Having understood our ultimate goal it is necessary for us in our journey to discuss the way to that goal. This topic needs an independent book. But here we shall try to review briefly the most important points assured that our readers who take their lives seriously will follow this journey through further studying and reflection.

Before anything we should pay attention to two points:

We should observe our goal constantly during our lives, day and night; otherwise we cannot utilise our power for our aim and the ordinary affairs will capture our attention and gradually it may make us doubtful about the necessity of following that aim. It is all too common for human beings who are not successful in their pre-decided program to try to get rid of their difficulties through a denial of that program.

We should pray and ask Allah seriously to help and save us. We cannot continue this spiritual journey without His special help. Yes, with His help there will be no obstacle and nothing can stop us. So in the relationship with Allah we should not feel self-sufficient, because we are completely and absolutely dependent on Him. However in the relationship with others we should trust ourselves and rely on our powers without allowing despair to capture our hearts. The Prophet (S) who was the bravest man and stood against all enemies and was able to change the world said:

"O My God! Do not ever leave me by myself even for an instant. "

Let's listen to Imam Sajjad (AS) when he asks Allah for help:

"Glory be to Thee! How narrow are the paths for him whom Thou has not guided! How plain the truth for him whom Thou hast guided on his way! My God, so make us travel on the roads that arrive at Thee and set us into motion on the paths nearest to reaching You!"

"Make near for us the far, and make easy for us the hard and difficult! Join us to Thy servants, those who hurry to You swiftly, knock constantly at Your door, and worship You by night and day, while they remain apprehensive in awe of You! You have purified their drinking places, taken them to the objects of their desire, granted their requests, accomplished their wishes through Your bounty, filled their minds with Your love, and quenched the & thirst with Your pure drink"

The right path towards our happiness is worship, servitude. Allah says:

"Did I not charge you, O children of Adam, that you should not serve the shaytan? Surely he is your open enemy, and that you should serve Me; this is the right path." (36:60,61)

The prophet Jesus (AS) also told the children of Israel:

Self-Knowledge

"Surely Allah is my Lord and your Lord, therefore serve Him, this is the right path." (3:51)

Worship does not necessarily mean special kinds of worshipping. Every action or even thought which is done for Allah's pleasure is considered as a worship. The worship in this broad sense is able to occupy all our life. Our works or jobs, our speaking or listening, our eating or drinking and even our sleeping can be for His pleasure and can be helpful in our spiritual movement.

We studied during our discussion about the goal of the creation that human beings are created to worship Him and that it is to their own benefits. We knew that there is a hierarchy of goals and we understood the place of worship, as one goal within the hierarchy.

If we want to worship Him and get close to Him, it is not enough to practice some prayers or fasting and the like. It changes all aspects of our being. First of all, we should know Allah and His religion. Secondly, we should obey those laws (act according those laws). Thirdly, we should make our characters and spiritual qualities as He pleases. Thus, there are three realms of improvement: creeds, deeds and virtues.

What should we do in respect to our creeds? According to Islam every person is asked to investigate religion. One should think, reflect, study and discuss religion. Some religious beliefs are necessary for all people, such as the main principles and some are not necessary for all people. So it is not necessary nor expected, that every person must know al the details about, say, the resurrection through personal investigation.

To make an inquiry into religious beliefs one should first of all depend on one's reason. After realising the truth of the religion or the Prophet (S) one can use the guidance of the Glorious Qur'an and traditions of the Prophet for further studies. Moreover the Prophet (S) has wanted all Muslims to refer to his household for understanding the real interpretation of the Glorious Qur'an and his pure tradition. The Prophet said:

"I leave two precious things among you that by grasping them you will never go astray after me: the Divine book and my Household. And they will never separate from each other until they come to me near the fountain (kawthar). Be careful how you behave with them after me."

This tradition is one of the traditions which expresses the authority of the Household of the Prophet in presenting pure Islam. Here is a list of books recording this tradition, but we should note that these are just some samples of Sunni scholars' works and there are many other books by Shi's and Sunni scholars which include this tradition: Sahih Muslim, the Book of fadail (merits) of Ali ibn Abi Talib, Vol. 7, p.122, Sahih al-Tirmidhi, Vol.5, p.328, Khasais a by Imam Nesa'i, p.21;

Musnad by Imam Ahmad ibn Hanbal Vol.3, p.17; Kanz al-'Ummal, Vol. 1, p.154; Al-Tabaqat al-Kubra by Ibn Sa'd, Vol.2, p.194; Jami' at-Usul by Ibn Athir Vol. 1, p.187; AI-Jami' al-Saghir by Al-Suyuti, Vol.1, p.353; Usd al-Ghabah by Ibn Athir Vol.2, p.12; Tarikh al-Dimashq by Ibn 'As5kir, Vol.5, p.436.; AlTafsir by Thn Kathrr, Vol.4, p.113.

We should take care of our beliefs: basic ones and derivative ones. if a person is not expert or skilled in discovering Islamic thoughts and concepts through the Glorious Qur'an or the traditions he must not interpret them according to his desires or weak understanding and he must not rely on those people who are not of sufficient knowledge and expertise. To use their books or sayings is like taking medicine according to the prescriptions of false physicians. Thus, understanding the details of the beliefs is like understanding practical laws.

According to Islam our happiness is not only based on our faith or beliefs. Deeds as well as virtues bear on our happiness. Islamic practical laws are to guide us in the realm of actions especially when our intellect or conscience is uncertain. Every person can learn jurisprudence and the related sciences and become a mujtahid. Then he can rely on his own understanding of the laws. But it is a difficult process and needs much cleverness, long work and practice. Those who are not prepared for this job have two other possibilities.

They can exercise precaution. For example, when they are in doubt about whether something is obligatory or recommended they must do it, or when they do not know whether something is forbidden or allowed they must not do it. To behave in this way is very difficult and even impossible for those who are not learned in jurisprudence. The second possibility is to imitate or follow a person who is proved to be a mujtahid or the most learned and at the same time just, trustworthy, insightful and the like. This kind of reference, i.e., the reference of a nonlearned to a trustworthy and learned person is advised by reason and approved by Islam. This is what we do in our daily life, e.g., we take the prescription of our physician or we ask some architect to make a plan for our house and so on.

There are also social duties for us especially in the present situation of the Islamic world. if we want to have respect in this universe and rewards in the other it is not enough' to perform our personal duties. Another role of that insightful, learned and just mujtahid is to declare the duties of the Muslims. Our intellect tells us that through obedience to this authority we can guarantee our material and spiritual happiness. Let's quote what Allamah Muhammad Rida al-Muddaffar has written in his precious book Aq'id al-mamryah:

"We believe that a fully qualified mujatahid is a representative of the Imam, in the case of the latter's absence. Thus, he is an authority over Muslims and performs the functions of the Imam as regards judgement and administration among the people...

Therefore the qualified mujtahid is not only one who issues fatwas, but he also has general authority over Muslims who must consult him if they require judgemen4 this being obtainable only from him. It is correspondingly wrong for anyone to give judgement except him or one who is appointed by him, as noone can pass sentence without his permission. "

After understanding our duties through taqlid (imitation) we should try our best to perform them. The first step is to perform the obligatory ones. if a person disobeys the obligatory duties he stops his movement towards Allah and even goes downwards. The second step is to perform the recommended affairs (mustafiabbdt).

Besides the performance of obligations we should take care of our spiritual qualities. This topic is studied in ethics, akhliq. To speak briefly, first of all we should recognise our bad qualities. Then we should try to get rid of them. In this way we can clean our spirits from all badness and make our hearts capable of receiving divine illuminations. Besides general ways there are some special ways to treat moral weaknesses particular to each of them. This process should be accompanied with acquiring good attributes and virtue.

These are outlines of the Islamic program for human beings to reach their happiness. We hope that the reader will allow these points by him or herself. It's nice to finish our discussion with two traditions of the Prophet (S):

"Most of my people enter Paradise through piety and good behaviour. They improve cities and lengthen lives."

"I have been sent to complete noble characters."

The Importance of Knowledge in Decision-Making

In our previous discussions we came to the conclusion that human beings are not the same; some are good and highly respected because of their own decisions and deeds and some are bad and worse that animals, again because of their own decisions and deeds. The last topic, "Free-will", was selected in order to reject all the excuses expressed by unsuccessful people who want to shift the responsibility completely to others or to the society or the environment or the like.

In the present discussion we want to understand those factors which bear on our decision-making or will. We may divide them into three categories: knowledge; desires and inclinations; power and ability.

If something is unknown to me and I do not have any information at all about it, I can never decide to do it. Let's consider a simple example. Suppose you want to buy a certain book. What kinds of knowledge do you need?

You should know your need. What kind of book do you need?

You should know your desire and favourite style of writing.

You should know and consider your background in that aspect or realm. How much do you know about that subject? To what extent you can proceed with the subject? If you are a student of high school, you may not make use of book which are written for experts on math or physics.

You should know where to find and buy books.

You should know the content, the style, the writer and the price of the book which you want to select and buy.

If you have complete knowledge but you do not have any desire to read or have books you will not decide to buy. Thus, the importance of the second factor is clear. Also the importance of power is clear. if you feel that you cannot do something you will not decide to do it. All actions require some kinds of power. Now let us turn to our own case.

On the way to perfection human beings are equipped with desire. All have some degree of self-love, so they desire and make efforts for their well-being, for a better future. Yet, they often make mistakes in deciding what is really better for them. Human beings also have power to follow the path to perfection. Yet, they are different in the amount of power they have spiritually, mentally and physically. For example, some can understand facts or decide what to do much better than others. Some can resist sin much easier than other people. Some are very respected and honourable and are not attracted to temporary material interests easily. Some are very healthy in their bodies so they engage in more voluntary fasting to obtain greater spiritual rewards.

All these differences are natural. Indeed, they are necessary demands of this material universe. But we should know that according to Islam, rewards or punishments and their amount are and will be decided in consideration of man's power and abilities. if someone has really no power to understand or to act according to Islamic rules, he is excused and Allah is most generous towards him. This group are very small in number. Most of people are wise enough and also sufficiently able to understand and follow the right path toward their perfection, although they actually possess different amounts of power and ability. Allah, the Wise, takes these differences into His consideration. He expects more of those who are given more talents or abilities than others. Generally one of the principles in His judgement is:

It means the most precious deed is the most difficult one. If a person needs more time to learn how to pray or to memorise verses of the Glorious Qur'an, his rewards will be greater and Allah will help him more.

Thus, human beings generally have no difficulty in power and desire or inclination which are needed in every decision and.. action. But what do you think of the third factor, knowledge? Most difficulties arise from a lack of knowledge, from ignorance. Now let's see which kinds of knowledge we need in our journey towards His pleasure.

Here is a list of facts which we should know:

We should know ourselves. How are we created? Why? What are our needs? What are our real desires or motives? What are our faculties and abilities? Are there any tasks or duties for us?

What is our present situation? Under what conditions do we live? How is our life in this universe? Is it the only life that we have? Is there any eternal life for us? What good or bad qualities do we have?

What is the best position for us? What values and goods can we acquire? What is a perfect man like?

What are the results of our deeds? What is the effect of this single decision or even intention on our fate? Generally, how can we transit from the present situation to the favoured and ideal one?

We can summarise these necessary kinds of knowledge as: knowing our origin, knowing our present, knowing our nature, and knowing their interactions.

There is a famous tradition from Imam Ali (AS) which is closely related to this discussion. Imam Ali said:

Thus, every person needs to know his origin, his present, and his future. Having acquired this knowledge one can behave and manage his life properly. Otherwise he cannot plan for his life because he has not acquired the necessary knowledge for deciding his goals and his way of life. For example, if I did not believe in the Hereafter and eternal life, my goal might be something to be obtained in this world. Or if I did not believe in the relationship between my actions and my happiness on the Day of Judgement, I would not care about my actions. If I believed that I was created through chance and not by Allah, the Wise, I would lose my hope in His help and mercy and would lose my confidence.

Therefore we will speak of the following subjects successively:

Our origin

Our present

Our future

The Ultimate goal

How to reach our goal.

Our Origin

One of the most fundamental things for a human being on the way to perfection to know is that he is created by Allah for a certain purpose. There are different approaches to this matter. In Islam every person is first of all invited to study this problem and make a certain judgement about it. Nothing less than certainty of belief in Allah is acceptable. There are different ways to prove the existence of Allah and a variety of reasons. But according to Islam it is not a difficult process to understand that Allah, the One, is Existent. Every one; at every level of knowledge and understanding, can settle this problem easily. Usually when a person is a disbeliever it is because of his will, although there might be rare cases of people who have studied this problem seriously and who were really longing for the truth, but they could not find it. Usually, atheism is just an assumption. Observe the following verse:

"Is there doubt About Allah, the maker of the heavens and the earth?" (14:10)

In Islam every value is due to the relationship with Allah. Our happiness is based on our voluntary devotion to Him. It is like the lives of plants and animals which depend on the light of sun. The sun does not need them, but they cannot survive without the sun.

Thus, we should change the common approach to Divine law or commands. They are not some boring duties assigned to us by Allah in exchange for His favours or His services to us. We are not to perform His commands in response to His blessings. We should know that His commands are only for our benefit. His religion, His prophets and His laws are the most precious blessings that we have ever received. Even thankfulness to Him (shukr) is for our benefit.

"And when your Lord makes it known: If you are grateful, I would certainty give to you more." (14:7)

If we are thankful, we increase our capacity to receive more blessings. With more thankfulness, again more blessings will be brought. It is an endless process. If we are not thankful, it is not harmful to Allah, but decreases our capacity for receiving His blessings, so we loose some blessings and if we continue, we will loose more.

We should always recall that He is our Lord, that our real happiness and freedom can be achieved only with our obedience to Him. There are only two ways: to be servants of Allah or to be servants of others such as oppressors or unjust governments or idols. To satisfy Allah is easy, because He is the One and He only wants our happiness. He never makes mistakes and never wants impossible things. But disobedience to Allah leads us to try to obey many gods, although it is not possible. If one wants money and fame and good position and comfort and the like, no matter how much of them he acquires, he will never be satisfied.

'Allah sets forth an example: There is a slave in whom are (several) partners differing with one another, and there is another slave wholly owned by one man. Are the two alike in condition?" (39:29)

If we think deeply we will understand that those different and conflicting gods are really our own different extreme desires. So there are two ways : to be servants of Allah or to be servants of our devious soul.

"Have you seen him who takes his low desires for his god? will you then be a protector of him?" (25:43)

"Have you then considered him who takes his low desire for his god, and Allah has made him err having knowledge." (45.23)

Finally, consider the true story which happened during the time of Imam Musa al-Kazim (AS). Once Imam (AS) was walking in a lane. When he was passing by the door of one house, Imam knew that there was some celebration there in which dancing and forbidden music and wine were used. Then a slave-maid opened the door and came out to put the garbage outside. Imam asked her: "Is the owner of this house a slave or a free person?" She answered: "Free". Imam said: "Surely he is free, because if he were a slave, he would fear his life and would not make such a session.

When the slave-maid returned, the owner asked her why she was late. She answered that a man with such and such appearance was passing and questioned me and I replied to him in this way. The owner was shocked and began to think deeply about this sentence: "if he were a slave, he would fear his lord." Suddenly he stood up and without putting on his shoes he went out of the house and looked for that man. When he reached Imam (AS) he repented. This man was Bushr ibn Harith, given the title of 'hafi', meaning shoeless. He became a real believer.

Our Present

Having discussed our origin, it is necessary to study our present situation and our future. Now let us turn to the former and the latter will be our topic in the next discussion. In order to certify our goal and practical program to reach that goal, we should know our qualities, capacities, abilities, opportunities and so on.

These are articles of our knowledge about our present. We have studied some of them in the previous chapters such as: good attributes of human beings, the vices attributed to human beings and free-will. Here we just mention some other aspects of our present situation.

Complete dependence

In our being (existence) and our life, we are completely dependent on Allah, our Creator. This existence and life is given to us by Him; We are not self-existent. We cannot survive without His will. We are also dependent on material conditions. We cannot exist without water, air, food, light, a certain temperature, and so on.

We cannot have a comfortable life without the help of other members of the society. No one can produce for himself whatever he needs of clothes, shelter (house), furniture, etc. With the progress and development of human societies these needs increase. Thus, we are dependent on our Creator and his blessings in the material universe and in the social universe.

In our knowledge and understanding, we are not needless.

With his God-given intellect every human being is able to understand many facts such as the truth of the religion and the existence of Allah and to acquire some easy and simple information about the nature and the environment around him. I With his God-given conscience, every human being understands) the general rules of morality, e.g., justice is good and oppression is bad. This theoretical and practical knowledge is common between men in primitive societies and men in advanced ones.

But what; makes us different from those ancient (earliest) people is what we have received from the prophets, especially the Noble Prophet of Islam, the seal of the prophets, whose message is the last and the;; most perfect message of our life and what we have received from the past generations. These two sources, religion and inherited knowledge, are very important. They serve as the point of departure for every field in the sciences, arts, literature, technology and positive laws (contracts) which have become very complicated, developed and advanced. For example, today when a chemist starts to work on a project, he uses the results of previous discoveries and inquiries. Many of those achievements have become trivial. Perhaps university students today know more than chemists in the 18th or even 19th century. Or in Islamic sciences, today we use many works on different subjects made by great scholars in the past centuries. Without them we would have to start from the beginning. But we are still on the way. What we know is much less than what we do not know.

Thus, we are completely needful and dependent in our existence, our life and our knowledge. We should not be proud of ourselves. We should not think we are needless or that our knowledge and understanding are perfect.

Mortality of this universe

This natural universe (dunya) is not eternal. It has started at a certain time and will reach to its end at a certain time. This earth, the sun, the moon and all stars and planets will be destroyed before the resurrection. This fact is expressed by many verses of the Glorious Qur'an such as the following:

"When the sun is covered, and when the stars darken, and when the mountains are made to pass away, and when the camels are left untended, and when the wild animals are made to go forth, and when the seas are set on fire, and when souls are united," (81:1-7)

Therefore, everything in this universe has a certain end. Our bodies are mortal. Our physical lives, our powers, our youth, fame and beauty are mortal (perishable). Allah is eternal and the spiritual (abstract) universe is also endless. Our spirits belong to the spiritual universe and not to the corporeal universe.

'And they ask you about the spirit Say: The spirit is from the commands of my Lord, and you are not given ought of knowledge but a little." (17:85)

And if we notice that our spirits make our personality and reality, we easily come to the conclusion that death is not our end. Death is like a gate to another universe. Not only our spirits but also our characters and acts will be preserved. (In the next chapter we will discuss the embodiment of our actions.)

Thus, we cannot obtain eternity and infinite life or endless pleasure in this world. if we want them, we should know they are due to the relationship with Allah. Because Allah is eternal, everything is related to Him (in a narrow sense), is of His signs, and shows Him and so, must be like Him.

"Everyone on it must pass away And there will endure for ever the face (wajh) of your Lord, the Lord Of glory and honour." (55: 26,27)

"And call not with Allah any other god; there is no god but He; every thing is perishable but His face (wajh); He is the judgement, and to Him you shall be brought back" (2:88)

In Arabic "wajh" is that part of any thing through which you can confront that thing. For example if you confront the foot or hand of a person, you are not confronting and meeting him, but when you confront his face and have a kind of face to face sight, you confront and meet him. This is why in Arabic our face is called "wajh". In the case of Allah, we know that He has no body, so it is not necessary to look in a special direction to meet Him. In the Glorious Qur'an this fact is expressed in the following verse:

"And for Allah is the East and the West, therefore, whither you turn, thither is Allah face Surely Allah is Ample-giving, Knowing." (2:115)

As we can consider and use everything to know Him, to reach Him, so every thing can be called "wajh Allah". Those things which are considered in this way will never be destroyed as we saw in the verses: (55:26,27) and (28:88). So every action or even intention which you have for His pleasure will be preserved. if you give some money to a poor person, this money will be destroyed but that aspect of this money or in other words that aspect of this action which is "wajh Allah" will be preserved forever.

True nature of this life

This present life in itself is one of the blessings of Allah. It is the only opportunity that we have. If we want to purify ourselves we should utilise it in the best way. Every moment of this life is so precious that no price can be considered for it. There is a famous tradition from the Noble Prophet(S):

"Whoever has not made any improvement in one day has lost "

In many prayers from our Imams we find the request for a long life. On the other hand, the Glorious Qur'an teaches us that disbeliveers who do not believe in His religion and the day of resurrection are afraid of death. They wish they could live for a thousand years or even more.

"And you will most certainly find them the greediest of men for life (greedier) than even those who are polytheists; every one of them loves that he should be granted a lift of a thousand years, and his being granted a long he will in no way remove him further off from the chastisement, and Allah sees what they do." (2:96)

Thus, both believers and disbeliveers like to live, but their reasons and their attitudes towards death and life are completely different. Disbeliveers or those who claim to be believers but do not practice the faith enjoy this life because they think that there is no other life or because they have not obeyed Allah and have committed sins or crimes, so they are afraid of His punishment. These people like this universe and this life just themselves. They are engaged in a circular life. They work to earn money, to buy food and clothes and to prepare a shelter for themselves. And if we ask them: Why do you need food and so on? They will Say: "Otherwise, we cannot work; we cannot live."

But for real believers this universe is precious because they can reach His pleasure, they can worship Him. The only opportunity for human beings to act and to improve themselves is in this life. After death, we cannot perform new acts. Today we can act and there is no judgement (reckoning) and tomorrow there will be judgement (reckoning) and no action. It is possible to do something in this life which will continuously bring His rewards. For example, if a person builds a school or hospital or the like with pure intention or if a person spreads his knowledge through teaching or writing or the like or if he has trained good children he will receive more and more rewards after his death. But it is obvious that even in these cases, there is no chance for acting after death.

Therefore, this life is very valuable. According to Islamic traditions, one of the first questions on the day of the resurrection is about the life, as another question is about youth. It shows the special importance of this period of life. To see a clear picture of the Islamic attitude towards life, it's nice to consider this prayer of the fourth Imam (AS):

"And Let me live as long as my life is a free gift in obeying You, but if my life should become a pasture for Satan, seize me to Yourself before Your hatred overtakes me or Your wrath against me becomes firm!"

And to get a clear picture of the ordinary attitude towards life, one may consider this verse of the Glorious Qur'an: 'That this world's life is only play and amusement and adornment and boasting among yourselves, and a rivalry in the multiplication of wealth and children, like the rain, whose causing the vegetation to grow, pleases the husband men then it withers away so that you will see it become yellow, then it becomes dried up and broken down; and in the hereafter is a severe chastisement and (also) forgiveness from Allah and (His) pleasure; and this world's life is naught but means of deception."

Without faith, this life can be divided into five parts. Some scholars consider these five parts in a chronological order, so they are five succeeding phases. During the childhood the main activity is playing 'la'ib'. Then it is the turn of 'lahw', including all the activities a person does just to enjoy himself in his free time or, in other words, just to make himself busy, like listening to music or watching movies or solving puzzles or collecting things or reading novels without any purpose or aim. Then when a person becomes young and ready for marriage, he or she takes care of his or her body and hair and generally his or her beauty.

He or she spends much time in front of mirrors or in the barber shops or in the cloth-shops. This is the period of adornment, 'zfrzah'. Then when he or she becomes graduated and finds a job and gets married, starts to exalt himself or herself over others and to be proud of himself or herself. This is the period of 'tafdkhur'. And finally after trying his best and working for many years he or she thinks about the results of his or her life: children, money, property and fame. He wishes to be the best. This is the period of 'takdthur'. This verse shows that we should not forget our happiness in the Hereafter and we should not allow ordinary affairs deceive us and capture our attention. Otherwise we will be lost in the chain of trivial wants and activities such as playing and so on. This part of our discussion will conclude with a phrase from Imam Ali (AS) about the Godwary, 'muttaqrn':

"They endured (hardship) for a short while and in consequence they secured comfort for a long time. It is a beneficial transaction that Allah made easy for them. The world aimed at them but they did not aim at you. It captured them but they were freed from it by ransom."

The Representative of Allah on Earth

We mentioned previously that one of the good attributes and values of human beings is the possibility of being caliph or representative of Allah on His earth. This is the highest value or perfection that one may reach. Because of the importance of this subject we should speak about it more.

The term khalffah literally means that which comes after another a successor. For example, a new generation is khalffah of the old one.

"But there came after them an evil generation, who wasted the prayer, and followed lusts; so they shall encounter error"
(19:59)

Those people who were rulers after the Prophet (S) were called 'khalffat al-raslll', meaning successor of-the Prophet, such as Imam Ali (A.S.). So what does 'Graiffat Allah' mean? Every person chosen by Allah to be His representative on earth is called Caliph. They are chosen by Allah to lead people, to judge between them and to guide them, because it is not possible for all people to receive Divine laws by themselves or to judge.

One of the verses in the Glorious Qur'an about this position is the following verse.

"O Dawud! Surely we have made you a viceroy (khaflfah) in the land; so judge between men with justice and do not follow

desire, lest it should lead you astray from the path of Allah;
(as for) those who go astray from the path of Allah, they shall
surely have a severe punishment because they forgot the day of
reckoning." (3:26)

This verse was revealed after a certain event. God wanted to test Dawned. The story is expressed in the previous verses, i.e., 21-25. Finally Allah made him His representative on earth and then a judge. According to the monotheistic view of the Glorious Qur'an no one has authority over people and the fight to judge among people, unless assigned or approved by Allah.

If someone is knowledgeable, it does not mean he can judge. Allah has the fight to judge and He appoints prophets. Prophets can also appoint others. There are many traditions of our Imams in which they explain that a person who has some qualities such as justice and ability to understand Islamic laws directly (ijtihad) can also judge as they are appointed by the Imams. So, there are two types of appointment: General appointment which is due to the possession of certain qualities, and special appointment in which some particular person is appointed and his name is mentioned.

So Dawud was one of the representatives of Allah on earth. Another case is found in the following verse.

'And when your Lord said to the angels, I am going to place
in the earth a khalifah, they said: what! Will You place in it

such as shall make mischief in it and shed blood, and we celebrate Your praise and extol Your holiness? He said: surely I know what you do not know." (2:30)

Here, a question arises that when God appointed a khalifah (according to the verse 2:30), was that appointing exclusive to Adam (A.S.) or not? The answer is negative. As we saw before Dawud (A.S.) was khalifah. Certainly Moses, Jesus, the Noble Prophet (S) and some other prophets were also khalifah. Some scholars use the following verse as one of their reasons to prove that it was not exclusive to Adam (A.S.).

"And He is who has made you successors in the land and raised some of you above others by (various) grades, that He might try you by what He has given you." (6:165)

Now let's go back to the verse 2:30. When we observe what the angels said, we find out that the appointment was not exclusive to Adam, because they said: "What! Will You p/ace in it such as shall make mischief in it and shed blood... ?" Those angels could not be afraid of Adam (AS). And if this position given to human beings was not so important, they would not protest or question Allah and they would not say: "What! Will You place in it... and we celebrate Your praise and extol Your holiness?"

So this is the conclusion: Allah wanted to appoint representatives of Himself on earth. The angels understood firstly, that this position is very high, secondly, that it was not exclusive to Adam (A.S.), and thirdly, that Allah wanted to make a new species on earth and among them some will be good and some will be bad and amongst those good human beings will be some at this high position (caliphate) and they will be rulers on earth or the natural universe. As a result, the angels wished that they had that closeness to Allah, because they were aware of their own goodness and they observed only negative points of human beings. Answering them Allah said: '1 know what you do not know". When Allah wanted to show the angels the merits of human beings, He taught Adam (A.S.) all the names. Let's follow this part of the problem through the following verses.

'And He taught Adam all the names, then presented them to the angels; Then He said: Tell me the names of those if you are right" (2:31)

"They said: Glory be to You! We have no knowledge but that which You have taught us; surely You are the Knowing, the Wise." (2:32)

"He said: 'O Adam! inform them of their names. Then when he had informed them of their names, He said 'Did I not say to you that I surely know what is hidden (ghayb) in the heavens and the earth and (that) I know what you manifest and what you hide?" (2:33)

So at least one of condition of being khalifah of Allah is conclusive knowledge. According to Shi'ism all the fourteen infallibles had this knowledge. We say: "Peace be with you, O representatives of Allah on earth."

When a person is chosen to be khalifah, he at least has one of two types of guardianship:

Guardianship over the universe and creatures. Having this kind of guardianship one can do everything in this world such as reviving the dead, curing the sick. It is called 'generative guardianship.

Guardianship in judgement and making Jaws. Ordinary people can never make laws. Even a mujtahid can not make any law and his job is just to refer to Islamic sources and understand practical laws. Also Islamic parliament can not make some laws instead of Divine laws. They try their best to apply general laws to different situations and if they make some laws, they are really filling empty places in the legislative universe which is delegated to them by Allah (to the people or to the legal authority). This kind of guardianship is called 'legislative guardianship'

According to the verse (38:26) Dawud (A.S.) had this kind of guardianship. Adam (A.S.) was khafffah on earth while perhaps there was no need for laws or judgements (for a further discussion of the very point look at comments on the verse 2:21). So at least his actual guardianship was generative. But after deeper study it will be obvious that every representative of Allah was allowed to apply his guardianship in both aspects: generative and legislative, if necessary and possible.

The Spirit

Having understood the importance of the spirit (Ruh) and the spiritual life, it is natural to pursue our discussion with this topic, the spirit. The issue of spirit is one of the oldest problems confounding the human mind. Even the earliest human beings were aware of a non-material entity within them. They were aware of different states and levels of consciousness in their lives, and by comparing sleep and death with their normal awake state reached some preliminary conclusions. They were also cognisant of the fact that humans are different from animals, with the latter lacking free will and wisdom. Animals just seemed to follow their instincts. They also thought about dreams. Dreams which came true were especially intriguing. Without being able to articulate it, they had an inkling that this might be the result of a part of the Person taking leave, traversing the future.

As human societies developed, such problems were delegated to philosophers who were good at thinking and reflecting. Philosophy confronted the issue by first asking: Is the spirit material or non-material? In other words, is this phenomenon part of our bodies or not? Material things have specific properties, for instance they can be divided into smaller parts which can also be divided into parts once more, ad infinitum, if the means were available. They also knew that if a person lost a limb, he or she was essentially the same person, with a handicap. Their notions of themselves did not seem to suffer in the process. Thus, many philosophers concluded that the soul is independent of the body.

This theory was further strengthened when they considered the notions of "I", "mine" and "me", as distinct features of the person. Is the person, this unit of a human being, material or non-material?

As noted with the loss of limb example, philosophers knew that humans even after losing parts of themselves were the same. We all seem to have an understanding of ourselves as a whole, as something which is not divisible, and which is simple and not compound. When we get our hair cut, we do not feel any less afterwards. That which remains besides our body and is not on the floor of the barbershop is what we are after.

Let us use another example to help clarify this illusive topic. When a person commits a crime, especially a heinous one such as masterminding mass killings, as the Nazis did in WWII, he is expected to be brought to justice, even if he committed the crimes half a century ago.

Science tells us that the average person's body cells are nearly all renewed every six years. For all practical purposes we are not physically the same person we were, say ten years ago. Why then should the Nazi officer, whose body bears little resemblance to the one which carried out the atrocities, be apprehended, tried, and punished? We intuitively understand that we are not losing some parts of our being which must be replaced.

The unity of identity which we feel is not justified only through physical continuity.

So there seems to be universal recognition of the fact that, what animates a person is ultimately constant, and is held responsible for the whole of the person body and spirit. Because the two are so closely interwoven, and because we humans are so deeply anchored in this physical, material world, we tend to identify with the body rather than the spirit. In Islam there is no doubt that the spirit is the essence of the person, and the body a vehicle for the manifestation of the soul in this world, and a means for its works.

There is a set of reasons proving the existence of the spirit through the study of our knowledge. If we prove that our knowledge is not material, it will be clear that we are not merely bodies. For example, it is obvious that a greater thing cannot be placed in a smaller thing. A big box can easily accommodate an smaller one put into it. The reverse does not hold. Then imagine gazing at a beautiful forest for a while, savouring all that stands before you. Later on when you remember the experience with all its grandeur, little thought is given to the size of the forest, which is, in a way, now stored within your memory. Whatever one might call it the idea, picture, or the experience of the forest fits neatly within a person's mind which is rather limited in size. We wonder how a forest, with all its characteristics and size can fit into our consciousness.

The problem is not solved if we imagine small microfilms, for instance, which are pictures of what we see, and are in one way or another, stored in our minds. Even extremely small microfilms have dimensions, which, when added together, would soon leave no more room in our minds for anything else. Also when you have microfilms you are in need of some means to be able to interpret those microfilms, You also need some ability to understand things in their real sizes. There is a difference between seeing a small picture of a forest and seeing the forest itself.

This is a rather difficult issue which has puzzled many of scientists. As a matter of fact, when a survey of top scientists, including Nobel laureates, was conducted recently, the vast majority, when asked what will be the most important field of research in the next decade, gave psychobiology as the answer.

It is somewhat well understood that neurones in our brains, through sensors, spread out like roots, pulses, electrical signals, if you will, by which they interact with billions of other cells. Brain waves are this measured, charted, and studied. Yet the nature of information storage is not well understood.

The repeated actions of a person, for instance an athlete after intense training which involves repeated motions of the same kind, do indeed leave physical traces in the physiology of the brain; as a stream of water would after running down the same path for a while. This enables the athlete to perform extremely difficult tasks without "thinking" or great effort at co-ordination. Yet this explains only part of the process. This is the wiring system, so to speak, and not the process of cognition, information storage, and retrieval. In what form the athlete's skills are stored is still not understood.

The question occupying many minds is: Is the physical brain the gateway unto something else, or is it all there is, and the end Of all that has to do with cognition? I hope we have understood how to answer this question without being engaged in technical discussions of philosophy. There are many other ways to prove that knowledge is not material. For example, knowledge is not changeable, but every material. thing is. For instance, today is Saturday. You have the knowledge that you are reading a book on self-knowledge this day. This knowledge is true today. When you think of it tomorrow, it will be the same. Your knowledge about this particular book will be the same after a week, a year, or say even twenty years after. When you forget something what this really means is that particular data have been lost which cannot be easily retracted tom the memory storage. By no means does it mean that your knowledge has altered.

Let us consider another situation. For instance, you have a friend whom you met two years ago. You have formed his image in your mind. When you think of that particular encounter, his mage crosses your mind with precisely the same details. Nothing has affected the image of your friend in your brain. If you were to turn into him on any given street now, you would still identify your friend with the same image that you had previously stored in your brain, If any metamorphosis took place within that particular acquired knowledge, you would not be able to recognise him.

However, you should know this fact that no data is lost at the unconscious level of your mind, even if you cannot recall some of our memories. It is important that you realise that the data have been safely stored in your memory. Whatever forms of experiences you have had in your life, they are in your memory. Now, in order to enable you to recall or extract those data, you need some mental training and practice. We will not elucidate this matter at this stage. What we want to say is that it is possible to lose knowledge at the conscious level of understanding and it is possible to feel that knowledge has become faded. For example, the details of the image of that person may be lost, but you still remember him to be that person. This shows knowledge is not material, because all material things change.

It is true that a huge solid mass of a substance cannot be fitted into or occupy a small vessel, a container or a receptacle, and so is the fact about our knowledge which can neither change nor be segmented in small portions. All these facts prove knowledge is not material. Therefore, we as owners of that knowledge cannot be material. It's not possible to suppose we are material, as we are owners of a non-material thing, the knowledge.

There is yet another way of proving this fact. Let's ask ourselves whether a material thing like a pen has knowledge about itself or about the external world around it. You will definitely say no. We know, for instance that the outer surface of a pen is not at all aware of its inner surface, or vice versa. The same condition applies when we talk of the relation between two or more pens. Therefore, it is irrelevant to say that these are the Parts of the same pen; or for that matter, these parts are of one book; the book is not one single thing. It is made up of many things, many atoms which are gathered in something which, is apparently one but not really one. Even if it were one it would have no knowledge about itself.

In the excerpt of late Imam Khomeini's historical letter to Gorbachev (31/12/1988), the Imam raised a philosophical point on material and non-material worlds. The late Imam drew Gorbachev's attention to the logical comparison of the soul, a non-material entity, and a statue, a material entity. Imam Khomeini was of the opinion that not everything could be analysed and justified through matter. Therefore, Imam Khomeini asked Gorbachev to consider for instance a

The Spirit

statue which possesses no knowledge. Every side of the statue is hidden from the either side.

This should be discussed philosophically, but it can be understood without this. So, a material thing has no knowledge about the entirety of its being and it also has no knowledge about the external world. But this is not the case with human beings. A human being has knowledge about himself, even when thinking about a problem in philosophy, mathematics, history, etc. When you have awareness about yourself, then, you also have awareness about the external world.

There are also experimental reasons to show the existence of the spirit. I am sure you have heard quite a bit about hypnotism. It is related to the invocation of one's soul to do something. Hypnotists make a person go to sleep, and then he gets that person to do something. The hypnotist is able to ask the person under hypnosis to execute his orders. For example, he can ask him to go back ten years and explain what happened when he was at school. He can even get the medium to speak a language he does not know; or sometimes hypnotism is exploited as an instrument to find out what is happening in other places, For instance, a person under the influence of hypnotism is sent to his place of residence and asked to describe what his or her mother is doing. The medium gives a detailed description and then the mother is asked to describe what she has been doing at that particular time, and her

102

description fits with that of the medium. Hypnotism is also used to cure some mental disorders. It can also be used as a means of entertainment.

This is not to say that every person who claims to have such an art is capable of doing so. Their claims may not be genuine. They may pose as impostors who would like to swindle some money out of some simpletons. However, hypnotism as a science and practice cannot be rejected because of the fact that it has some applications in the field of medicine to cure some forms of mental derangement.

There is something else called spiritualism not in the sense of philosophy but a branch of science in parapsychology. People claiming some powers of spiritualism say that they can summon the spirits of the dead through a medium. For example, the spirit of a person's grandfather who died two or three decades ago can be summoned through a medium to speak to him. The spirit can be asked to give the exact location of something like the lost picture of the grandmother. He can even be asked to give the details of his murderer in some mystery murders. It has been proved that some of these stories disclosed by the medium have been found to be authentic.

It is said that today more than a hundred magazines are published around the world on the subject of spiritualism by the spiritualist societies. All of them believe in the existence of the spirit and they claim that they can have contact with the spirits. I do not want to say that all of them are true, but this fact cannot be ignored.

It is better to give examples from the lives of our own scholars. Allamah Sayyid Muhammad Husain Tabatabai the author of AlMizan a great commentary on the Glorious Qur'an (20 volumes), had a brother, who was called Sayyid Muhammad Hasan Ilihi, and this brother was also one of the great scholars. Ilahi had a student who was able to summon spirits. However, his brother did not disclose that he practised this parapsychological science. It is a custom among great scholars to observe and keep low profile in the areas where they have extraordinary supernatural powers. Ilahi, the brother of Allamah Tabatabai said that at times he had some questions and problems in the comprehension of some ideas in philosophy and he needed to discuss those problems with the original source. His student used to come to his rescue by recalling the spirits of great philosophers and through him, Ilahi used to clarify and solve the riddles in philosophy. But his student was not aware of those solutions since he was not a master of philosophy.

It is interesting to observe that a real arif (gnostic) can easily control supernatural phenomena and can even attain a rank where he can control everything in the universe. However, he considers these things of no importance. These practices are within the reach of students of ifran (mysticism). The gnostic masters consider these attainments as very elementary and rudimentary. Those who possess high mystical ranks can easily read your mind. They can predict the events taking shape in totally different surroundings precisely. Therefore, it is not strange that the student of Ilahi was able to summon the spirits.

Siyyed Jalal al-DinIn Ashtiyani gave a special interview, published in Kayhun Farhangii. In the interview, Allamah Ashtiyani said that once he had contact with the spirit of Hakim Sabzevari who recited a couplet of Mawlawi from the Mathnawr which could not be found in the copies at Allamah Ashtiyani's disposal. Finally, through studies, Allamah Ashtiyani learned that a man from the West had found a copy of the Mathnawi which contained the couplet.

So this phenomenon of being able to make contact with the spirit of the dead is a very common practice. It bears no special weight and is insignificant to our scholars and our ulama. They do not, at the same time, want to speak about these matters because they say that if they did so, it would cause some unnecessary complications. They do not want to resort to such practices to avoid publicity as well as people's harassment. Consequently, they try to cover these facts. Only the closest friends may become aware of these practices. This issue may be raised in public for very specific purposes on very rare occasions.

The late Imam Khomeini was skilled in 'irfan in theory and practice. However, he never gave himself the airs of possessing such an insight. Only some of his students who were in his service related some things about him. They even confessed that they had difficulty in perceiving those aspects of his mystical practices. The Late Imam was an 'arif of a very special rank. He possessed such high traits that he never bragged about himself nor did he attribute any special quality to himself. The great Imam Khomeini was an arif in the real sense. The Imam has left a treasure of works in the field of irfan.

Ifran is divided into two major branches. There is practical ifran and theoretical ifran Theoretical irfan is treated as a science whose subject matter is Allah. Practical irfan studies how to get close to Allah and what the stages on the mystical journey are. Those skilled in these branches have studied many things in irfan They can teach it, but there exists a possibility that they may not be practising arifs It may be due to the fact that they have not reached certain station on the mystical journey. Perhaps they are ordinary beings merely in possession of some knowledge which they can transmit on mysticism.

Having both the practical and theoretical knowledge Simultaneously, if put into practice, leads us towards understanding Almighty Allah's Infinite Wisdom and His Endless Attributes to be able to be honoured with His everlasting blessings to His most amiable lover, His most obedient servant and His complacent slave if our soul totally submits to His Will, and His Injunction.

We have earlier discussed the subject of spirits. We proved the existence of the spirit as a non-material reality. We also said that it is our spirit or soul which makes our personalities, and the body is not as important as the soul. The body is just a receptacle or carcass that carries our spirit. Sometimes the scholars and philosophers compare the body and the spirit to a mount: a mule or a horse. Our soul intimately co-ordinates with our body and effectively uses it as a means in the performance of different tasks.

It is possible for the soul to reach a position and a stage where it becomes totally independent of the body. This stage can be materialised as a reality once a person begins to strengthen his soul through worshipping Allah, his obedience to Him, and the performance of religious duties. If one persists in these practices, his dependence on the material world will decrease as his soul progresses towards the Divine kingdom through his spirit's sanctification. Thus, his soul gradually alienates itself from the physical body.

Many of the mystics and great scholars were able to experience ethereal travel. They would sometimes look at their own bodies. For example, some reported that when they saw their bodies for the first time they thought that they were looking at another person, but after a while they understood that they were looking at their own corporeal bodies.

A very famous and respected scholar from Mashhad, Mirza Jawad Aqa Tehrani(c. 1919-1989) in one of his books says: "The best reason to prove the existence of the spirit) is to see the spirit out of the body. This is for those who had this opportunity and I once have personally seen my spiriti.e., myself before my body just as I now see myself before my clothes which I have taken off and are before my eyes. "

This scholar was very religious and committed, and his son relates that his father was once sitting in the yard and after a while he stood up and went to his room. After a while he come back. His son asked him why he returned. He said that he had seen some ants on his clothes and realised that they were from the yard and he was afraid that had he returned to the room, those ants would have lost their way. Consequently he came back to the yard to put them back in the same place. Then he returned to his room. It can be concluded that these pious people took care of every detail of their minute actions to attain the lofty positions and special spiritual ranks.

We can deduce that it is not at all difficult to prove the existence of the spirit as we did in our previous discussion. We can now draw this conclusion that since our spirits are "on-material, and since our personalities and our real entities are principally shaped by our non-material spirit, our comprehension of the knowledge of the self clearly demonstrates that we should emphasise our spiritual needs more than our material needs. Evidently, we should focus more on the spiritual side of the self than on our corporeal body.

The Status of Human Beings in the Glorious Qur'an

We can look at human beings from two different angles. The first view would be to explore human beings as a whole in general terms; or else we can deal with the matter by looking at them as individuals. The Glorious Qur'an presents both aspects. Sometimes the Glorious Qur'an speaks of human beings in general terms. At times, it treats the matter on an individual basis, for example with the presentation of the Pharaoh as a bad person. It also sometimes speaks of good people like the wife of Pharaoh, the prophets and so on. So, both aspects are thoroughly dealt with in the Glorious Qur'an.

Now we want to speak about humans generally, not some individuals, but as a whole. Can we understand from the Glorious Qur'an that humans as a whole are good or bad? What is the answer? As a whole can we say something?

According to the Glorious Qur'an a human being can be the best and the most perfect creature. As far as our knowledge permits, we recognise, comprehend and identify these beings according to given norms. If we compare man to any form of matter or living things such as plants and animals and so on, we will immediately draw an important conclusion that human beings are better, more intelligent and perfect. If man can cultivate a field and make use of the produce for his own and others' benefit, capture animals, make use of them and extract natural resources for upgrading his life and that of the society, naturally, we definitely come to this result that man is a higher being. For instance, an elephant is much bigger than a human, but man trains it and controls it to do some work for him.

Thanks to his talents, physical abilities, mental powers, and the indomitable spirit that Almighty Allah has bestowed upon man, his life has adjusted according to the needs of his time and place. For example, the way of life today is completely different from that of the ancient ages. Again, when we compare the ancient way of life with that of life in the stone age, you will see that man has always been after improvement. The change of the mode of life can be studied in context with that particular age of man. However, this is not the case with the animals. All the animals have followed the same pattern of survival for centuries. The environment may have modelled their pattern of survival but they have never been the masters of the environment. Many animal species have become extinct due to environmental changes. Human beings have shown their capability to survive by modifying their environment to fit their needs. Consequently, we can say that man is more perfect than animals. Would it be wrong to conclude that man is the best creature?

We can say yes, and we can argue for it in some ways, but we should be careful! When we give an affirmation of our status, it does not mean that every human being is better than every other creature!

Are human beings better than the angels? We do not want to speak about one person. Yes, the Prophet of Islam (S) and Imam Ali (AS) are better than any angels. That is clear. But can we make a generalisation that a new-born child is better than an angel? It is difficult to say because the actual perfection that a child has is not sufficient to answer this question, but we can argue for the idea in other ways.

According to a verse from the Glorious Qur'an we can deduce that man is very important and precious.

"Then we made the life-germ a clot, then we made the clot a lump off lesh, then we made (in) the lump of flesh bones, then we clothed the bones with flesh, then we caused it to grow into another creation, so blessed be Allah, the best of the creators."
(23:14)

This verse explains different stages of creation that a human being goes through. After the body achieves its perfection, Allah, the Most Glorious, gives him another creation. What it means here is that Allah, the Creator, bestows souls into the body. This is the final phase of creation. On the first day the embryo has no spirit, then after some months, Allah the Glorious breathes life into the foetus. So we can realise why Allah the Almighty has emphasised the stage of creation of the spirit by saying 'another creation' which means that the spirit is not an ordinary thing of the material world. The spirit belongs to another heavenly universe.

When people were asking the Prophet (S) about the spirit and its nature, the following verse was revealed. The answer was that the spirit is from the command of Allah(1) or that it belongs to the abstract world (according to different interpretation, but the result does not change).

'And they ask you about the spirit. Say: The spirit is from the command of my Lord, and you are not given ought of knowledge but a little." (17:85)

Notice that in the last part of the verse (23:14) Allah, the Almighty, says: "Blessed be Allah who is the best of the creators". According to this verse of Scripture, we can now conclude that man is the best creature. Because it is the best Creator who can create the best creature. To understand this point more perfectly we should take note of the following verse:

'And surely we have honoured the children of Adam, and carried them on the land and at the sea, and provided them with good things, and we have made them to excel by an appropriate excellence over many of those we created." (17:70)

Since Almighty Allah has honoured man with the highest position on the earth and has bestowed upon him the highest respect, the Creator provided man with the means to excel many but not all of His other creatures. What this sentence really implies is that there may be some creatures superior to man, otherwise Allah would have pronounced thus: We have made them to excel over all of our creatures. Now the question arises whether man can be considered the best creature.

Man can rise to the rank of supremacy if he makes use of his God-given possibilities. Man progresses on the ladders to supremacy according to his possibilities. These God-given possibilities are the natural or Divine gifts (talents) innate in every being. These talents are of two kinds: actualities and capacities (potentialities) for further perfection. Our corporeal body, being the first dimension, is, to some extent actualised at the time of our birth. But it is not the case with our soul which is the other dimension.

Every individual is capable of reaching the highest level of perfection; they can be vicegerents of Allah; they can be the real servants of Allah. These capacities or potentialities, (although dormant at the time of birth) excel in quality compared to every other creature. Natural gifts do not make us better than other creatures at birth.

However, when we opt for the right path to develop our Godgiven talents and begin to fully make use of the potentialities bestowed upon us, we start climbing the ladders to supremacy. The more constructively we make use of those potentialities, the better we become compared to other creatures. We can ascend to the ranks that no angel has reached. And if man takes a wrong path and begins making use of the God-given talents in a wrong direction, man can descend to the murkiest level where no animal has fallen!

We can conclude that at the time of birth, because of our innocence and purity we may excel many creatures, but there are some creatures like angels who are better than us at that particular stage. Yes, human beings are equipped with the best talents and are made in a manner that can reach the highest levels possible for a creature. So Allah's power and wisdom is best manifested in human beings. That is the reason that Allah says:

"Blessed be Allah, the best of the creators."

Now let's return to the Glorious Qur'an to see the values of human beings. We will give a list of attributes beginning with the good attributes of humans and then the bad attributes. There are many verses and it is not possible to mention them all.

The Vices Attributed to Human Beings

We can describe man in two different ways. We can view man in general terms as masses or speak about some individuals. When we say an individual is good or bad, it does not imply that all are bad or good. It does not mean that the same qualities can be attributed to all human beings. If an individual happens to possess an undesirable quality, that stain can be cleansed through strengthening his faith. Here we want to mention some undesirable attributes of human beings mentioned in the Glorious Qur'an

Man is unjust and ignorant

These two qualities are expressed in the following verse:

"Surely he is very unjust, very ignorant" (33:72)

Two qualities, man being very unjust and his being very ignorant are expressly emphasised. In Arabic there is a difference ilm, and alam. A zdlim is a person who commits sin, even if only once, but according to Arabic grammar zalam (RA) is said to be the exaggeration form of zallim It means a person who frequently commits unjust actions. Also, jahul is the exaggeration form of jahil. It means a person who is very ignorant or completely unwise.

Human beings suffer from ignorance and injustice. The unjust act is not restricted to others. It can be applied to the person himself.

"Every person who breaks Divine laws, has oppressed himself" (95:61)

If a person does not pray or fast then he has been unjust to himself. When a person beats someone or robs him of his money, he is initially doing a disservice to himself, then to the other person. Committing a sin is just like drinking poisoned water. Now if this person drinks poison, he is hurting himself. The same logic can be applied when he harms another being. The consequences of his ill acts would be his destroying the bases of his inherent God-given purity. He initiates hindrances on the way to his perfection.

Man is ungrateful

This fact is expressed in the following verse:

'And it is He who has brought you to life, then He will cause you to die, then bring you to life (again); most surety man is very ungrateful"(22:66)

According to Arabic Kr basically means to cover. example, if a farmer places seeds in the ground, this action is called kufr. The term has been used later for two other meanings which were likened to the root meaning (to cover). These two are:

To disbelieve in Allah or his religion.

To be unthankful relating to the blessings of Allah (the Almighty).

When a person is given health but misuses it or thinks it is not from Miab, this person is a kafir and if he is very ungrateful he is kaffir. This meaning is meant by the above verse.

Man is often unthankful and ungrateful. He quickly becomes oblivious to the blessings of Allah, the Beneficent. We read in the Glorious Qur'an the story of Korah (Qarun). He had so much money kept in the treasury safes that it took a large number of the keepers of the treasures who had difficulty carrying the keys of his treasury:

"We gave him [Korah] from the treasures to the extent that keys were difficult to be carried by a group of people possessed of great strength." (28:76)

Korah was invited to be thankful to Allah for innumerable bounties that the Almighty Lord, the Beneficent, bestowed on him. They invited Korah to make use of the blessings and perform good deeds to attain a station of piety and bliss in the next abode (the

Hereafter) as God has bestowed upon him His favour. However, the ignorant and arrogant eyes of Korah could not perceive the divine Blessings. In return to this invitation he said:

"I have been given this only on account of the knowledge I have." (28:78)

Korab was finally punished by Allah. Allah made the earth swallow him up and his abode. Those who yearned for his place only the day before began to say:

"Ah! (Know) that Allah amplifies and straitens the means of subsistence for whomsoever he pleases of His servants; had not Allah been gracious to us, He would most surely have abased us; Ah! (know) that the ungrateful are never successful" (28:82)

Man is an inordinate being

This fact is expressed in the following verse:

"Nay! Man is most surely inordinate, when he sees himself free from need." (96:6,7)

Human beings feel self-sufficient when they enjoy the status of wealth, health or position. When a man has no money or social position or is not from an important family, he is not inordinate. To illustrate, one of the companions of the Prophet (S) was quite poor. He asked the Prophet (S) for help. He gave him some money. That money was blessed and had good effects. Day by day his money increased. He used to pray behind the Prophet (S). But as his money increased, his worship decreased. The Prophet (S) began to feel concerned about him. So, one day he asked that man to pay the money back. When he paid it back, his money was no longer blessed. He became poor again and started to attend the mosque regularly and say his prayers behind the Prophet (S).

Man is hasty and does not have sufficient patience

This fact is expressed in the following verse:

'And man prays for evil as he ought to pray for good and man is ever hasty." (17:11)

Therefore if one wants to be patient, he will have to train himself.

Man shows total reliance on Almighty Allah, the Omnipotentonly when he is in trouble and difficulty When men's difficulties disappear their reliance also diminishes. They think they have become self-sufficient. This fact is expressed in the following verse:

'And when affliction touches a man, he calls on Us, whether tying on his side or sitting or standing but when We remove his affliction from him, he passes on as though he had never

called on Us on account of an affliction that touched him."
(10:12)

For example, before examinations students observe all the religious rituals and try to be close to Almighty Allah, but once the examinations are over, the feeling of being close to the Lord, the Creator, wanes.

Man is a niggardly being

This fact is expressed in the following verse:

"Say: if you controlled the treasures of the mercy of my Lord, then you would withhold (them) from fear of spending, and man is niggardly." (17:100)

Man is a greedy being

This fact is expressed in the following verse:

"Surely man is created of a greedy temperament; being greatly grieved when evil afflicts him, and niggardly when good befalls him, except those who pray, those who... " (70:19)

Man is an inquisitive and curious being

He is interested in discussing and arguing about everything more than needed. The Scripture presents such an idea:

The Vices Attributed to Human Beings

'And certainly We have explained in this Qur'an every kind of example; and man is most of all given to contention."
(1:54)

Up to now we have discussed nine bad attributes of human beings (although there are more). According to the Glorious Qur'an a human being is a responsible being and has the capability of either following right path or going astray. A man is able to choose either of these qualities, grow them, nurture them and strengthen them in his being.

The bad attributes or vices are not such that they can prevent a human being from reaching perfection, because the vices are of three kinds:

Some are necessary implications of his creation and he can not prevent them. For example, he is weak and has many limitations in his existence and actions. Allah, the Glorious and Most High, says:

'And man is created weak" (4:28)

This kind of attribute will not be questioned or punished. Allah just explains them to make us aware of our weakness and to prevent us from taking pride in ourselves. Some are implications of his creation but are not necessary. It means that his nature only inclines toward vice, but it can be resisted. To explain this point philosophically, we should say that his nature is not the sufficient condition or complete cause (al-illah altdmmah) of moral vice. It is just the incomplete or partial cause (al-illah al-ndqisah). It is lip to human beings to submit themselves to their nature or to resist. For example, growing up in a bad family tends to result in vice, but this is only an incomplete cause. Returning to our own discussion, the human being has a greedy temperament but he can control and direct his temperament to any direction he wants. He can even use it to acquire infinite perfection.

Some vices are caused by the human being himself, i.e., by his free will and are not due to human or individual nature. For example, if a human being is a liar, this is because he himself has chosen that.

Thus, we understood that the vices of human beings cannot prevent us from perfection and that Allah, the Most Merciful and Forgiving, will never punish us for those nature-given attributes. Man possesses of capabilities and potentialities as well as freewill. It is up to him to decide what to do or obtain. In the Glorious Qur'an Allah says:

"Most surely man is in loss, Except those who believe and do good, and enjoin on each other truth, and enjoin on each other patience." (103:2,3)

According to the above verses all human beings are in a state of loss, because they are losing their lives and their bodily and mental powers. The only exceptions are those who believe, do good and invite each other towards truth and patience. These people spend their lives or powers or properties to get divine pleasure and salvation. So what they get or obtain is more than what they spend or lose.

"Certainty We created man in the best make. Then We Tendered him the lowest of the low. Except those who believe and do good, so they shall have a reward never to be cut off "(95:4-6)

Again the same fact is seen. Allah has created man in the best way. Then it is up to him to be the lowest of the low or to be higher than other creatures, even angels.

It is obvious that not everybody known to be a human being is precious. Human beings are not at the same level. Therefore they should not be treated equally. For example, those people who create world-wars and perform many crimes are not to be respected at all. Really, they are not human beings (in spite of their shape or body). God-willing there will be an appendix on Islamic punishments. We will shed some light on this matter to meet objections against the Islamic system of punishment suggested by some Westerners who consider it incompatible.

www.ingramcontent.com/pod-product-compliance
Lightning Source LLC
Chambersburg PA
CBHW031428120626
46545CB00006B/2309